THE MASTERS

The Winning of a Golf Classic

THE MASTERS

The Winning of a Golf Classic

by Dick Schaap

WITH AN INTRODUCTION BY *Frank Beard*

A MADDICK MANUSCRIPTS BOOK

CASSELL · LONDON

CASSELL & COMPANY LTD
35 Red Lion Square, London WC1
Sydney, Auckland
Toronto, Johannesburg

Copyright © 1970 by Maddick Manuscripts, Inc.
All rights reserved. No part of this publication
may be reproduced, stored in a retrieval system,
or transmitted, in any form or by any means,
electronic, mechanical, photocopying, recording
or otherwise, without the prior permission of
Cassell and Company Ltd.

First published in Great Britain 1971

I.S.B.N. 0 304 93828 9

Photographs courtesy of William Sauro and Wide World Photos, Inc.
Manufactured in the United States of America

ACKNOWLEDGMENTS

The author would like to thank the following people whose reportage made this book possible:

DAVE ANDERSON
IRA BERKOW
GENE ROSWELL
BILL SEARBY
NICK SEITZ
MEL ZIEGLER

And, most of all, the man who coordinated the reportage:

DON FORST

All the photographs in this book—except a full-page picture of Gene Littler—were taken by WILLIAM SAURO, who, under the weight of cameras and film, doubled as an excellent reporter. The Littler picture is from Wide World Photos.

For Maury and Leah,

THE MASTERS OF CEDAR BROOK

CONTENTS

INTRODUCTION BY FRANK BEARD   xi

A PARTIAL CAST OF PLAYERS   xv

Sunday, April 5, 1970: *The Gathering of the Clan*   1

Monday, April 6, 1970: *Sizing Up the Course*   17

Tuesday, April 7, 1970: *The Fairways Grow Narrower*   39

Wednesday, April 8, 1970: *Tapering Off*   63

Thursday, April 9, 1970: *A Crystal Vase for the Bridesmaid*   77

Friday, April 10, 1970: *Three 68s From Three Continents*   105

Saturday, April 11, 1970: *The Missionary Moves Up*   135

Sunday, April 12, 1970: *Two In, Two Out*   169

Monday, April 13, 1970: *Out of the Woods*   211

APPENDIX   229

INTRODUCTION

During my first eight years on the pro golf tour, I've won ten tournaments, and I'd gladly give up any five of those titles to win the Masters. If pressed, I'd probably be willing to give up all ten. That's how much the Masters means.

The Masters is unique. The course is nowhere near the most difficult in the world, the field is certainly not the strongest and the purse is far from the largest. Yet, somehow, the Masters has a special kind of atmosphere every other tournament lacks. From the moment I enter the grounds of the Augusta National Golf Club, deep in Georgia, I feel as if I'm stepping into golf history.

It's a hard feeling to explain. Among the four major championships open to pro golfers—the Masters, the United States Open, the British Open and the Professional Golfers Association—the Masters is, by a wide margin, the youngest. It began in 1934, almost three-quarters of a century after the British Open, almost forty years after the U.S. Open, almost twenty years after the PGA.

Still, none of the other major tournaments gives me the sense of history, the sense of tradition, that I find at the Masters.

Perhaps it's because, of all the major championships, the Masters is the only one played every year on the same course. Or perhaps it's because the Masters was conceived, and inspired, by Bobby Jones, the only man to win the U.S. Open, the British

Introduction

Open, the U.S. Amateur and the British Amateur in a single year. Or perhaps it's because almost all the great golfers of my lifetime—Hogan and Nelson and Snead and Demaret and Palmer and Player and Nicklaus—have won the Masters and have produced so many of their most memorable rounds on the Augusta course.

I'm not the sort of golfer who lives only for championships, who feels he has to win or die. That's not my style. The closest I come to burning for victory is in April of each year, when I return to Augusta.

I'll never forget the first time I played at Augusta. It was in 1965, my third full year as a touring pro, and I got into a practice match with three former Masters champions—Henry Picard, Ralph Guldahl and Herman Keiser. All three were well beyond their prime, yet I never played a round of golf that went so fast. The three of them pointed out to me bare spots where trees had been leveled by lightning, where mounds had been erased. They showed me bunkers that had been moved, and they kept saying things like, "Now here's where I hit the shot that cost me the Masters in '37," or, "Now here's where I made the shot that won me the Masters in '39," or "Now here's where I had a putt to beat Nelson, and it just slipped off the edge."

And then Picard or Guldahl would line up the same putt and stroke it again and it'd slip off the edge again, and he'd shake his head sadly. I'm not a very sentimental guy, but it got to me—the Masters' blend of the past and the present.

It still gets to me. I walk into the antebellum clubhouse at Augusta, and I'm awed by the photographs on the walls—of Jones and Hogan and General Eisenhower. I stare at the picture of Gene Sarazen, in his outdated knickers, and then I turn and look in the locker room, and there's Gene Sarazen, in his outdated knickers, the winner of the U.S. Open seventeen years before I was born, getting ready to go out and play a round of golf.

. . .

Introduction

When I wander out on the Augusta National course, among the magnolias and the azaleas and the dogwood and the flowering peach, I can't help feeling that this is the way golf is supposed to be played. And I can't help hoping that someday I'll win the Masters, someday I'll put on the green coat of the Masters champion, and then I'll know that as long as I live, as long as the Masters survives, I'll be coming back to Augusta, playing golf on this course, in these surroundings, telling the new young golfers, "Now here's where I hit the shot that won me the Masters."

—*Frank Beard*

A PARTIAL CAST OF PLAYERS

TOMMY AARON:
Thirty-three years old, from Gainesville, Georgia, playing in his eighth Masters. Solid and steady, with a game well suited to Augusta. Belongs among the favorites, except for one disturbing tendency: Give him a chance to win, and he'll usually finish second.

FRANK BEARD:
Thirty years old, from Louisville, Kentucky, playing in his sixth Masters. Unspectacular but remarkably consistent, the leading money-winner on the 1969 professional golf tour. He hooks his drives, which helps at Augusta, but lacks the killer instinct.

BILLY CASPER:
Thirty-eight years old, from Bonita, California, playing in his fourteenth Masters. Twice the United States Open champion, winner of more than $1 million during his fifteen years on the tour. Finished in top twenty-four at Augusta nine times in the 1960s. Best modern golfer never to win the Masters.

A Partial Cast of Players

DAVE HILL:
Thirty-two years old, from Jackson, Michigan, playing in his third Masters. The second-leading money winner on the 1969 tour. Known for his chain-smoking, explosive temper and refreshing candor. A good long shot. Due to win a major tournament.

GRIER JONES:
Twenty-four years old, from Wichita, Kansas, playing in his first Masters. Named the rookie of the year on the 1969 pro tour. Considered one of the best bets among the professionals playing Augusta for the first time.

TAKAAKI KONO:
Thirty years old, from Japan, playing in his second Masters. Impressively accurate with his irons, possesses an exceptional short game. The only contender among the Asian professionals.

GENE LITTLER:
Thirty-nine years old, from La Jolla, California, playing in his seventeenth Masters. One of the smoothest swingers in golf, winner of more than twenty tournaments, including the 1961 United States Open, the fifth-leading money-winner of all time. Rarely has played up to his potential at Augusta.

BOB LUNN:
Twenty-four years old, from Sacramento, California, playing in his second Masters. Considered a threat because his power game is geared to the Augusta course.

STEVE MELNYK:
Twenty-three years old, from Brunswick, Georgia, playing in his first Masters. A big man and a big hitter, the 1969 United States amateur champion. The first amateur in years given a serious chance to win the Masters.

A Partial Cast of Players

JACK NICKLAUS:
Thirty years old, from Columbus, Ohio, playing in his twelfth Masters. The youngest man ever to win the Masters, the youngest to win it for a second time and the youngest to win it for a third time. His game is perfectly matched to the Augusta course. Automatically the favorite.

ARNOLD PALMER:
Forty years old, from Latrobe, Pennsylvania, playing in his sixteenth Masters. The first man ever to win $1 million on the pro golf tour, the only man to win the Masters four times. Still a threat on the course that brought him his greatest victories.

GARY PLAYER:
Thirty-four years old, from South Africa, playing in his fourteenth Masters. In 1961, became the first and, so far, only non-American to win the Masters. Has finished in top ten at Augusta nine times in twelve years, an unmatched record.

CHI CHI RODRIGUEZ:
Thirty-four years old, from Puerto Rico, playing in his seventh Masters. One of the smallest men in pro golf, yet one of the most powerful. A long shot.

DAVE STOCKTON:
Twenty-seven years old, from San Bernardino, California, playing in his second Masters. Given an outside chance because of his putting ability.

JIMMY WRIGHT:
Thirty years old, from Enid, Oklahoma, playing in his first Masters. A club pro, he finished fourth in the 1969 PGA championship. A very long shot.

A Partial Cast of Players

BERT YANCEY:
Thirty-one years old, from Tallahassee, Florida, playing in his fourth Masters. In his first three appearances at Augusta, finished third, third and thirteenth. He points his whole golf game—physically and mentally—toward winning the Masters. A strong bet.

SUNDAY

April 5, 1970

The Gathering of the Clan

They have come from all over to play in the Masters, from Taiwan and Thailand, from Latrobe and La Jolla, making the pilgrimage to Bobby Jones' tournament. They have come by invitation, but they qualified for their invitations by falling into one or more of fifteen categories:

1. All former Masters champions.
2. U.S. Open champions for the past five years.
3. U.S. Amateur champions for the past two years.
4. British Open champions for the past five years.
5. British Amateur champions for the past two years.
6. PGA champions for the past five years.
7. 1969 American Ryder Cup team (professionals).
8. 1969 American Walker cup team (amateurs).
9. The first twenty-four finishers, including ties, in the 1969 Masters.
10. The first sixteen finishers, including ties, in the 1969 U.S. Open.
11. The first eight finishers, including ties, in the 1969 PGA.
12. The first eight finishers, not including ties, in the 1969 U.S. Amateur.
13. One player, not otherwise eligible, either amateur or professional, selected by ballot of the former Masters champions.

The Masters

14. *Six professionals, not otherwise eligible, who have posted the best records on the PGA tour since the 1969 Masters.*
15. *A sprinkling of non-American players, professional and amateur, selected by the Masters tournament committee.*

Conceivably, if there were no overlap, more than 130 golfers might qualify each year for invitations to the Masters. But because so many men qualify in more than one category—Jack Nicklaus, for instance, earned a 1970 invitation in five separate categories, and even Miller Barber, who has never won a major title, qualified in four categories—the field generally ranges between seventy and ninety. The field this year is fairly typical—eighty-three players, fifty-four of them American professionals, thirteen American amateurs, fifteen foreign professionals and one foreign amateur.

These are not the eighty-three best golfers in the world. At least thirty of them, possibly forty, have no chance to win the Masters. They are the ornaments of the field—the venerable champions, the amateur collegians, the token Thai—their skills either tarnished by age or not yet polished by experience.

Still, the twenty-five finest golfers in the world are entered, with one notable exception: Lee Trevino, the brash and outspoken 1968 U.S. Open champion and the leading money-winner on the current tour, is missing. After he tied for nineteenth place in the 1969 Masters, his second shot at Augusta, Trevino announced, "It's just not my kind of course. With my game, I can't play there. They can invite me all they want, but I'm not going there any more."

A short time later, under pressure from the Professional Golfers Association, Trevino publicly apologized, saying that his remarks were not intended as criticism of the event or of the course. But privately, Trevino, a Mexican-American, burned. He was unhappy both with the course, which does not favor his

April 5, 1970

kind of straight, low-ball hitting, and with the social climate in Augusta, a Deep South attitude which does not make a dark-skinned Mexican-American feel particularly welcome in the town.

And when Trevino was tendered his invitation to the 1970 Masters, he declined. He said he had other plans for Masters Week.

On the eve of the Masters, Lee Trevino was the only golfer in the world heading away from Augusta out of choice.

6:55 A.M.

At the Sedgefield Country Club in Greensboro, North Carolina, Billy Casper trudges down the first fairway, unaccustomed to playing golf at such an early hour on a Sunday. The contenders in the final two rounds of every tournament tee off last, and almost always, when he enters a tournament, Billy Casper is a contender.

But yesterday Casper shot a lackluster 73, which gave him a total of 143 for the first two rounds of the Greater Greensboro Open and left him fully twelve strokes behind the leader, Arnold Palmer. One stroke higher, and Casper would have missed the cut. One stroke higher, and he would have been eliminated from Greensboro's last two rounds, both being played today because of a rainout Thursday.

Casper's game is not sharp, with good reason. For one thing, he skipped the entire Florida tour the month of March, in deference to his allergies. Casper is a festival of exotic allergies, most of them aggravated by the insecticides and fertilizers used on Florida courses.

For another, he is breaking in a new set of clubs, clubs with lightweight steel shafts, replacing woods he had used since 1957 and irons he had used since 1960. With the old clubs, Casper had won almost $1 million.

And, finally, he is tired. He and his wife, Shirley, flew to Washington, D.C., late yesterday afternoon to spend an evening with two other golfing families, the Arnold Palmers and the Richard Nixons.

On the final day of the 1969 Masters, Billy Casper teed off in first place, a stroke in front of George Archer. Casper had led after each of the first three rounds; he had broken par every day. Sharp and poised, he looked like a certain winner.

But then, on the front nine of the Augusta National course, Billy Casper shot a disastrous 40, four strokes above par. He rallied for a 34 coming in, but it was too late. He lost the Masters to George Archer by a single stroke.

"No, really," Casper, a devout Mormon, insisted afterward, "I'm not disappointed. It's just another experience in life."

8:05 A.M.

Jack Nicklaus sits in the Augusta National clubhouse, eating a weightwatcher's breakfast of half a cantaloupe, two eggs and one unbuttered slice of whole wheat toast. He has trimmed down to 191, a loss of nineteen pounds in six months. Neither his slacks nor his nickname, Fat Jack, fits him any longer.

"I want to get in my round early today," Nicklaus says. "I've got to fly home to Palm Beach this afternoon for my son Steve's seventh birthday party."

Nicklaus has played a practice round each of the past three days. "How'd you do yesterday?" someone asks him.

"Shot a 69," he says, "but I played badly."

Only Jack Nicklaus can play badly at Augusta and shoot a 69.

In 1966, for the first time in a decade, no one broke par for the seventy-two holes of the Masters. The tournament wound up in a three-way tie, at 288, among Tommy Jacobs, Gay Brewer and Jack Nicklaus.

When Nicklaus won the playoff by two strokes, he com-

April 5, 1970

pleted the most remarkable four-year record in Masters history. From 1963 through 1966, he played seventeen rounds at Augusta and shot only three rounds above par. In 1963, at the age of twenty-three, he became the youngest Masters champion. In 1964, he finished second. In 1965, he tied the eighteen-hole record of 64 and set a tournament record of 271, breaking Ben Hogan's mark by three strokes. And then in 1966, with his play-off victory, he became the first man to defend successfully a Masters title.

Someone suggested, after the 1966 Masters, that the course be retired and presented to Nicklaus. After all, he had shown that he owned it.

The following year, Jack Nicklaus shot a 79 in the second round and missed the cut.

8:15 A.M.

Arnold Palmer and Gary Player approach the first tee at the Sedgefield Country Club, ready to start their third rounds in the Greater Greensboro Open.

Palmer, the halfway leader at 131, hasn't hit a shot, but he is already weary. After his round yesterday, he hopped into his personal jet, flew home to Latrobe, Pennsylvania, picked up his wife, Winnie, flew to Washington and then, after joining Billy Casper at the White House dinner honoring the Duke and Duchess of Windsor, flew back to Greensboro. He got only four hours' sleep.

Player, tied for third place at 133, feels fresh. At thirty-four, six years younger than Palmer, and after a good night's sleep, Player isn't fazed by the prospect of thirty-six holes. "I'm an athlete," he says. "I can go seventy-two holes in a day if I have to."

They tee off, trailed by the early-rising division of Arnie's Army, the fanatics who cheer every swing Palmer takes, and by Gary's Guards, a squad of plainclothesmen assigned to protect the South African from racial protests. Ever since Arthur Ashe, a black American, was refused permission to play tennis in South Africa, Player has been a target for civil-rights activists in the United States. Repeatedly, Player has argued that sports and politics should be separated, but his critics—South Africa's critics—do not agree.

Rumors are already circulating that a major protest will take place in Augusta.

At the start of the final round of the 1956 Masters, Ken Venturi held a two-stroke lead. As the day turned out, all he would have had to do was shoot a 78 to become the first amateur to win the Masters. Instead, he shot an 80 and finished second, a stroke behind Jack Burke, Jr.

Four years later, Venturi, by then a professional, sat in the Augusta clubhouse, watching the finish of the 1960 Masters on television. He had completed his four rounds in 283, five under par. Only one man could catch him: Arnold Palmer, still on the course, four under par with two holes to play. Palmer needed one birdie to tie, two birdies to win.

On the seventeenth green, Palmer rolled in a thirty-foot putt for a birdie.

On the eighteenth, he rolled in a six-footer for a birdie.

The two birdies did much more than win Palmer his second Masters championship. They made "The Palmer Charge" a permanent part of golf's vocabulary, and for the millions of TV viewers who saw the putts drop, they established professional golf as a dramatic, compelling, big-time sport.

Palmer, who had won his first Masters in 1958, came back to win the event again in 1962 and 1964, giving rise to a theory that Arnie would always win the Masters in even years.

In 1966, he finished two strokes out of first place.

In 1968, he missed the cut.

April 5, 1970

9:30 A.M.

To Bert Yancey, a former West Point cadet, the Masters is the most important golf tournament in the world, the one he wants to win more than any other. "A month before the tournament," his friend Frank Beard has said, "Bert goes into his Masters fog. That's all he thinks about, all he dreams about—the Masters."

As he works on the putting green at Augusta National, Yancey smiles happily. "Everything before the Masters is just shadow-boxing," he says. "I never feel like playing golf until I get here."

Yancey grew up in Tallahassee, Florida, less than 250 miles from Augusta. "But I made up my mind, when I was a kid," he says, "never to go to the Masters until I received an invitation to play in it. And I never did. I never even was in the town of Augusta till I played in the Masters three years ago."

"Never in Augusta?" a reporter asks.

"Never," says Yancey.

"Not even accidentally—on the way somewhere?"

"Sir," says Yancey, with great patience, "Augusta isn't on the way to anywhere."

Not once, since the second year of the tournament, had anyone won the Masters the first time he played the Augusta course. But in 1967, Bert Yancey, a rookie in the Masters, took the first-round lead with a 67, held the halfway lead at 140 and, after three rounds, shared the lead at 211 with Julius Boros and Bobby Nichols.

But in the final round, Gay Brewer, who had lost in a playoff the previous year, shot a 67 and captured the green jacket. Yancey faded to third.

The following year, in the final round, Yancey shot a 65 and climbed into third place with a seventy-two-hole total of 279.

The Masters

Ironically, a score of 279 would have won the Masters either a year earlier or a year later.

10 A.M.

The United States Amateur champion, Steve Melnyk, who is called "Fluff" because he is six-foot-one and weighs 240 pounds, waits to tee off on the first hole at Augusta National. "I've been here since Thursday," he says. "Shot a 69 yesterday, but it doesn't mean anything. It's just practice."

Melnyk grew up in Brunswick, Georgia, some 150 miles south of Augusta. He has never played here before, but he has perfect breeding for the turf. The year before he was born, his mother won the Georgia Women's Amateur at the Augusta Country Club, which adjoins Augusta National.

Melnyk graduated from the University of Florida, and so far, has resisted the temptation of professional golf. He has joined the executive training program of a life insurance company in Florida and says he would like to remain an amateur.

"I probably have more incentive to win here than the pros have," says Melnyk. "It'd be a wonderful thing for the game. The amateur ranks have been hurt by so many good young players immediately turning pro when they get out of college."

Melnyk smiles, an easy, pleasant smile. "Wouldn't it be a great story if one of us amateurs won?" he says.

In the opening round in 1954, thirty-one-year-old Billy Joe Patton, playing in his first Masters, shot a 70 to share the lead with Dutch Harrison. In the second round, Patton shot a 74 to take the lead all by himself, one stroke ahead of Ben Hogan. No amateur had ever before been alone in first place in the Masters.

In the third round, Patton slipped to a 75 and third place, five strokes behind Hogan, two behind Sam Snead.

Against all logic, Patton refused to fold. On the sixth hole of the final round, he scored a hole-in-one and moved back into the lead. He held first place through the twelfth hole—the sixty-

April 5, 1970

sixth hole of the tournament—then slid back and wound up one stroke behind Hogan and Snead, the two greatest professionals of the decade.

Patton was the first of three amateurs to come within a stroke of the Masters championship—Ken Venturi in 1956 and Charlie Coe in 1961 were the others—and he was the leader of a remarkable group of amateurs in 1954. Of the top twenty finishers that year, five were amateurs (including Venturi and Coe).

Since 1962, no amateur has finished in the top twenty at Augusta.

1:10 P.M.

The third round of the Greater Greensboro Open is over, and four men share the lead—Arnold Palmer, Miller Barber, R. H. Sikes and Tommy Aaron. Gary Player is one stroke behind.

No one pays much attention to Aaron. He is paired with Palmer and Player, and between Arnie's Army and Gary's Guards, Tommy's Troops are practically invisible.

Aaron, like Steve Melnyk a Georgian who went to the University of Florida, is rarely noticed. After a decade on the pro tour, he is still looking for his first tournament victory in the United States. (He did win the Canadian Open last year.) It is one of the mysteries of professional golf, because few players are so gifted and so consistent as Tommy Aaron.

For five straight years, from 1965 through 1969, he has placed among the top fifteen at Augusta, an unmatched record. In those five years, he has shot ten sub-par rounds. But he has never finished within three strokes of the champion, and he has never held first place for even a round. His most common score is a 71—an accurate reflection of his game, efficient but quiet.

In 1968, Tommy Aaron escaped from anonymity at Augusta—for a reason he would just as soon forget. He went into

THE MASTERS

the final round three strokes behind the leader, Gary Player, one stroke behind his playing partner, a veteran Argentine named Roberto de Vicenzo.

Aaron played good golf that day, but de Vicenzo played incredibly. The Argentine shot a 31 going out and came to the last two holes six-under for the round, ten-under for the tournament.

On the seventeenth hole, de Vicenzo got a birdie.

On the eighteenth, he got a par.

Bob Goalby came in a few minutes later at eleven-under. Apparently, he and de Vicenzo were going to play off for the Masters championship.

But Aaron, keeping de Vicenzo's scorecard, marked down a par-four—instead of a birdie-three—for the seventeenth hole. Then de Vicenzo, still tense from the finish, signed the incorrect scorecard and handed it in. Under the rules of golf, the Argentine had to take the higher score—giving him 66, instead of 65—and had to settle for second place.

"Stupid, stupid, stupid," de Vicenzo kept calling himself in the press tent, after the most costly mathematical error in golf history became known.

Aaron quietly slipped away from Augusta.

2:30 P.M.

Jimmy Wright looks like a professional golfer. He is tall, six-foot-three, and slender, a handsome, friendly Oklahoman. He is the head pro at the Inwood (Long Island) Country Club, and in 1969, he won the Long Island Open, the Metropolitan Open, the Metropolitan Pro-Pro teamed with his assistant, the Long Island Pro-Am teamed with an Inwood member named Hank Cohen. These are not exactly titles that awe Wright's rivals at Augusta. But in the PGA last August, Wright

April 5, 1970

finished fourth—only three strokes behind champion Ray Floyd—to earn his first invitation to the Masters.

"I got here yesterday," says Wright, standing outside the Augusta clubhouse, "and just took one look at this place, and I felt like playing golf. I was fantastic. I hit sixteen greens in regulation. I felt terrific. The same thing today. Tee to green, I played just the way I wanted to."

Wright glances out toward the first tee. "I wish the tournament were starting tomorrow," he says.

2:45 P.M.

Early in the fourth round of the Greater Greensboro Open, R. H. Sikes, a slim, cheerful Arkansan, moves into first place, leading Gary Player by a stroke. Sikes has told people he needs a victory for the sake of Sir Winston. Sir Winston is Sikes' English bulldog, who is in the hospital, suffering from a mysterious illness.

3:10 P.M.

On the eighteenth hole at Augusta, the finishing hole that has provided more television drama than any six playwrights, Frank Beard pumps his second shot to within five feet of the pin. Then he knocks in his putt for a birdie, a nice way to complete his first 1970 practice round at Augusta.

"How you hitting 'em, Frank?" someone asks.

"The same," says Beard. "I'm just steady. I don't have any red-hot spells."

4:30 P.M.

In the clubhouse at Sedgefield Country Club, Gene Littler pulls off his spiked golf shoes. He has completed his two rounds, shooting 71 and 73, and he has finished at 284, not even good enough to make the top thirty in the Greater Greensboro Open.

"I'm not playing at all well," says Littler, shaking his head. "I just can't seem to hit the ball squarely. And playing thirty-six holes the Sunday before the Masters isn't exactly the best thing in the world."

A year earlier, going into the Masters, Littler was at the peak of his game, coming off a playoff victory at Greensboro and leading all money-winners with more than $90,000 in earnings. But this year, Silent Gene—"Gene the Machine," the man with as fluid a swing as exists in golf—has gotten off to a slow start. Going into the Masters, he has won less than $20,000.

Littler does not seem anxious to get to Augusta. Even when he is playing well, he does not enjoy being out on the tour. He makes no secret of the fact he would rather be home in La Jolla, relaxing with his family and tinkering with his fine collection of antique cars.

5 P.M.

Grier Jones and his wife, Jane, drive up to the Augusta National Golf Club for the first time in their lives. He missed the cut at Greensboro yesterday, then moved south today.

Jones parks his car and walks through the clubhouse, past the putting green, to the eighteenth green. He glances at the tenth fairway to his left and at the eighteenth fairway in front of him.

Then he turns to his wife. "Is it as tight as it looks?" he asks rhetorically.

Jones, the only rookie to finish among golf's top sixty money-winners in 1969, is normally a cocky young man. He stares again. "It looked a lot wider on television," he says.

5:45 P.M.

Gary Player wins the Greater Greensboro Open. He finishes with a 65 for a total of 271 and collects first-prize money of $36,000. Miller Barber finishes second, and R. H. Sikes third, while Arnold Palmer and Tommy Aaron fade to a tie for fifth.

For Player, the critical shot was a bunker shot on the par-five sixth hole. Forty feet from the pin, he popped the ball out of the sand and into the cup for an eagle-three.

April 5, 1970

"The sand blaster," says Player, at the press conference following his victory, "is the club I've won my tournaments with. I practice hours with it. Last year, on the tour, I was in bunkers ninety-two times and got down in two eighty-four times."

Player smiles. "I had no green to work with on that shot today," he says. "The only way to play it was to hole it out."

In 1961, Gary Player became the first man in the history of the Masters to shoot each of his first three rounds in the 60s. At the end of fifty-four holes, he was ten under par and four strokes in front of his nearest rival, Arnold Palmer. He seemed a cinch to become the first foreigner to win the Masters.

In the final round, Player's touch deserted him. He slumped to a 74 and came very close to a higher score. On the eighteenth hole, he put his second shot in a bunker to the right of the green.

But from the bunker, Player got down in two shots. He salvaged his par and finished the tournament at eight-under.

Moments later, Arnold Palmer came to the eighteenth hole nine under par, bidding for his third Masters title. He, too, put his second shot in the bunker to the right of the green. It took Palmer four shots to get down; he finished at seven-under. Gary Player's gifted sand blaster had saved him the Masters championship.

The following year, Player tied for first place at Augusta. In the playoff, he led Palmer by three strokes after nine holes—and lost by three strokes.

In 1968, he once more led the Masters going into the final round and slipped back to a tie for seventh.

For seven straight years, from 1959 through 1965, Player finished among the top eight at the Masters. The tournament made so deep an impression on him that he named his home in South Africa "Augusta."

11:10 P.M.

A few dozen soldiers, stationed at Fort Gordon, Georgia, wander around Bush Airport in Augusta, waiting for flights to take them home on leave.

An Eastern Airlines plane, from Greensboro via Charlotte, lands, and the passengers debark. A few of the soldiers do a double-take: They gape at an attractive young lady walking a schnauzer through the airport.

The young lady is Jeanne Weiskopf, a former Miss Minnesota and the wife of golfer Tom Weiskopf.

Weiskopf, who tied for second in the 1969 Masters, stands off to the side, waiting for his luggage, along with Tony Jacklin, the current British Open champion; Dave Marr, the 1965 PGA champion; and Julius Boros, twice the U.S. Open champion and once the PGA champion.

Jeanne Weiskopf and her dog draw all the stares. No one seems to notice her husband or Jacklin, Marr and Boros.

After all, in Augusta, in April, the sight of great golfers is hardly a cause for wonder.

MONDAY

April 6, 1970

Sizing Up the Course

The Augusta National is an awesome golf course. Not for its length: Even with its tees pushed back and its pins tucked in the far corners of the undulating greens, it is under 7,000 yards long. And not for its perils: Lightly bunkered, with broad fairways and sprawling greens, it is not nearly so difficult as the Colonial in Fort Worth or Firestone in Akron or Warwick Hills outside Flint, Michigan.

Augusta National is awesome for its beauty—a striking, natural sort of beauty, the fairways nestled among gentle valleys and flowering trees and sparkling streams, giving the terrain the same glitter as the contestants. No one who sees the course can escape the feeling that sometime before he dies, if his life is to be complete as a golfer, he must play here.

And Augusta National is a true test of golf, designed to reward the man who hits a ball the way it should be hit: Long and straight and, always, intelligently.

The course was laid out by Bobby Jones and a Scottish golf architect named Alister McKenzie, and their purpose, Jones once wrote, "was to provide a golf course of considerable natural beauty, enjoyable for the average golfer and at the same time testing for the expert player. . . . We want to make the bogeys *easy, if frankly sought, pars readily obtainable by standard good play, and birdies, except on par-fives, dearly bought . . ."*

Jones and McKenzie succeeded so well that a weekend golfer, a man who rarely breaks 100, can go to Augusta and shoot in the low 90s, thoroughly enjoying his game; and so well that, at the height of their careers, a Sam Snead could shoot an 80 and an Arnold Palmer and a Jack Nicklaus each shoot a 79.

Each of the eighteen holes at Augusta is named after the tree or plant that dominates its terrain, and each has its own special character:

No. 1: White Pine, 400 yards, par-four. An ideal drive, down the right side, must be long enough to carry a fairway bunker.

No. 2: Red Dogwood, 555 yards, par-five. A downhill hole, bending to the left. A long, hooking drive opens up a second shot to the green.

No. 3: Flowering Peach, 355 yards, par-four. An easy green to reach, a hard one to hold, set on a plateau and requiring a soft, delicate approach. One of three par-four holes at Augusta that has never been eagled.

No. 4: Palm, 220 yards, par-three. Another extremely difficult green to hold. The only par-three that has never been aced.

No. 5: Magnolia, 450 yards, par-four. A dogleg left, leading to a steeply rising green. He never yielded anything better than a birdie.

No. 6: Juniper, 190 yards, par-three. From an elevated tee to a multi-level green. A weak shot will back off the green into trouble.

No. 7: Pampas, 365 yards, par-four. Surrenders pars regularly, but stingy with birdies. No one has ever eagled this hole.

April 6, 1970

No. 8: *Yellow Jasmine, 530 yards, par-five.* Another dogleg to the left. The least treacherous of the par-fives.

No. 9: *Carolina Cherry, 420 yards, par-four.* Slightly downhill. A relatively simple par.

No. 10: *Camellia, 470 yards, par-four.* The start of the toughest three-hole stretch on the course. Demands a long drive and a precise shot to a green surrounded by trees.

No. 11: *White Dogwood, 445 yards, par-four.* The green lies, menacingly, in the bend of a stream, and only the boldest players bid for birdies.

No. 12: *Golden Bell, 155 yards, par-three.* Over water to a fearsomely narrow green. The wind can be a factor.

No. 13: *Azalea, 475 yards, par-five.* A stream protects the front of the green.

No. 14: *Chinese Fir, 420 yards, par-four.* A long drive down the left sets up a birdie possibility.

No. 15: *Fire Thorn, 520 yards, par-five.* A pond guards the green, allowing birdies only to the brave and strong.

No. 16: *Red Bud, 190 yards, par-three.* Over water to a deep green, shaded by trees.

No. 17: *Nandina, 400 yards, par-four.* A fairly routine hole, attacked best from the right side of the fairway.

No. 18: *Holly, 420 yards, par-four.* Uphill to a green sternly defended by bunkers.

On the first day of Masters Week, the players test the course. Some have been in town for days, acclimating themselves, but most were entered at Greensboro and are now getting their first 1970 look at the course. A few are getting the first look of their lives at Augusta National.

The Masters

The players go through the ritual of getting their yardages, stepping off the paces from appropriate landmarks—trees, mounds, bunkers—to the front, the middle and the back of the green. The golfers who have played Augusta before look for changes, made by man and nature, in the constantly evolving layout. The golfers who are making their first appearances get the feel of the course.

The course evokes respect. It looks peaceful, almost tame, but every man who is about to compete knows that one simple fact transforms Augusta National into a stroke-consuming monster: The knowledge that it is the site of the Masters, the knowledge that the man who best copes with the course gets to wear the green jacket of the Masters champion.

8:45 A.M.

Lionel Hebert, once the PGA champion, drives into the players' parking lot outside the Augusta National clubhouse. He is in his forties now and has not won a tournament since 1966. Yet he seems to save his strongest showings for the Masters. For three straight years, he has finished among the top eight here; he has shot only one round in twelve higher than 73.

If anyone should be able to withstand the pressure of the Masters, it is Lionel Hebert. "This is the only course I know," he says, "where you choke when you come in the gate."

9 A.M.

From the practice tee, Gene Littler is scattering his shots all over the range. Usually, he can put ten balls in a row on top of each other.

Littler frowns, waves his caddy in and goes to play a practice round.

"How you doing?" a California newspaperman asks the California golfer.

"I'm a basket case," says Littler.

April 6, 1970

10:30 A.M.

Gay Brewer, the 1967 Masters champion, is eating breakfast in the clubhouse. He spots Miller Barber entering the room. The day before, Barber had fairly short putts for birdies on each of the last three holes at Greensboro. If he had made two of them, he would have tied Player for first place; if he had made all three, he would have won the tournament. He missed all three.

"Hey, Miller," Brewer calls, with a friendly grin. "I see where you choked it."

Barber smiles back. He led the 1969 U.S. Open until the final round. "Same old story," he says. "Couldn't get a putt down when I needed it." Barber can afford to smile; he has won a quarter of a million dollars in the past three years.

10:50 A.M.

On the practice green, Frank Beard, one of the half-dozen best putters in the world, lines up a short putt, strokes it—and watches it roll two feet past the cup. "These greens are lightning," Beard says.

The greens at Augusta are traditionally fast; they demand a delicate touch and a keen eye, and a large share of luck doesn't hurt, either. The greens are cut twice each day, and as the tournament progresses, they get faster and faster.

"They're as fast now as they were on Sunday last year," Beard says.

11:15 A.M.

Gay Brewer and Miller Barber are working side-by-side on the practice tee, exposing two of the most unorthodox swings in professional golf. The stands behind them are filled with spectators, mostly people who do not have tickets to the tournament itself but who have bought one-day admissions to watch the golfers practice.

Brewer launches into his downswing, which features a very large loop.

"He looks like a man trying to kill a rattlesnake with a whip," says a reporter standing nearby.

Then Barber goes into his swing, his right elbow flying way out as he brings his club back.

"I think he's going to break his arm," says the reporter.

Brewer looks toward the spectators. "They won't get a show like this very often," he says.

11:30 A.M.

As Gene Sarazen emerges from the clubhouse, he is immediately spotted by two spectators, Mrs N. L. Armistad from Richmond, Virginia, and her sister-in-law, Mrs John Henry Smith of Augusta. Sarazen is easy to spot. For one thing, he is sixty-eight years old. For another, he is wearing rust-brown plus fours, a white turtleneck sweater and brown-and-white spiked shoes.

"My, just look at him," says Mrs. Armistad. "I love him."

"He's from another era," says Mrs. Smith.

In 1963, in the opening round of the Masters, Jack Nicklaus shot 74, Arnold Palmer shot 74, Gene Littler shot 77, Billy Casper shot 79—and Gene Sarazen, then sixty-one years old, shot 74. After a 73 in the second round, Sarazen was even with Palmer, still ahead of Littler and Casper—and the oldest man ever to make the cut at Augusta. He wound up in forty-ninth place in the tournament.

In 1969, at the age of sixty-seven, Sarazen shot a par-72 in the second round and missed the cut by only two strokes.

11:35 A.M.

Dan Sikes—no relation to R.H. Sikes—checks into the Town House Hotel with his wife, Marie. "I want a big room this week," he says. "When the Masters takes hold in a couple of days, you can't fight your way into these local restaurants.

April 6, 1970

I'll be taking a lot of meals from room service, and I want to have room to eat."

A non-practicing lawyer from Jacksonville, Florida, who didn't begin playing the pro tour until he was thirty, Dan Sikes is one of the brightest of the touring golfers—and one of the most outspoken. Some of his friends say he uses the clubhouse to keep in shape for the day he returns to the courtroom.

It's easy to tell Dan Sikes from R. H. Sikes. R. H. doesn't voice a lot of opinions.

11:45 A.M.

For his first practice round at Augusta, Grier Jones, the Masters rookie, teams up with two veterans—Gene Sarazen and Herman Keiser.

Keiser is fifty-five years old, and he has no chance to win the 1970 Masters. No one understands this better than his caddy, a New Yorker named Sam, who last year carried Tom Weiskopf's bag. "We tied for second," says Sam, using, like most caddies, the first person plural to describe his golfer's better efforts.

At Augusta, the caddies do not get to pick their golfers. They are assigned by the caddymaster; if a pairing works well, it can last for years. Sam looks at Keiser, then looks at the ground. "I got me a quarter-horse," says Sam, "and I need four quarters."

In 1946, Herman Keiser didn't have a chance to win the Masters. Nobody outside of the most avid golf fans had ever heard of him. When he teed off early in the morning for his first round, almost no one bothered to watch him. "It's no fun to watch me play," admitted Keiser, whose swing was far from classic. "In fact, it's painful."

But in the first round, Keiser shot a 69 and shared first place. Then, in the second round, he shot a 68 and moved five strokes in front of the field. In the third round, he shot a 71 and maintained his five-stroke lead.

Keiser faltered in the closing round, and when he three-putted the eighteenth hole, he finished the tournament at six under par.

Playing almost an hour behind Keiser, Ben Hogan birdied the fifteenth hole to move even at six-under. Hogan parred the sixteenth, then parred the seventeenth. He came to the eighteenth, needing a birdie to win. Ben fired his second shot to the green, only twelve feet from the cup.

Hogan lined up the putt carefully and stroked it toward the hole. It slid past—thirty inches past. Again, Hogan lined up his putt, and again, the ball slid past. He had three-putted.

Herman Keiser was the Masters champion.

"I'll be back every year," said Keiser, after his victory, "if I have to walk fifteen hundred miles to do it."

In 1969, Keiser shot an opening 71 and the next day, with a 77, survived the cut at the age of fifty-four.

12:25 P.M.

Australia's Bruce Devlin, a bright and pleasant man who was a master plumber before he became a master golfer, drives off the eleventh tee.

Two years ago, Devlin became the first man ever to shoot three out of four rounds at Augusta in the 60s—and not win the tournament. He shot three 69s—and a 73 in the second round. He would have had a 69 in the second round, too, except for a disaster on the eleventh hole.

He caught the water guarding the eleventh green, took a penalty stroke, splashed in again and wound up with a quadruple-bogey eight. A cautious par-four would have given him a 69—and the Masters championship.

"Of course, I think of that eight every time I play the eleventh hole," Devlin says. "It's hard to forget something like that."

April 6, 1970

His second shot bounces off to the right of the green, the safe side, away from the water. "I will never again play it toward the water," he says.

1:05 P.M.

On the fourth hole of his practice round, Bunky Henry, once a place-kicker for Georgia Tech, hits his tee shot just a few inches above a bunker guarding the green. He has to climb into the bunker to play the next shot, and as he puts his club down to address the ball, the ball rolls back into the sand and comes to rest against his right foot. He moves his foot and the ball rolls back farther.

"I've taken one swing," Henry yells to his partners, "and I'm laying five."

He has penalized himself one stroke for moving the ball, two strokes for touching the ball with his foot and one stroke for moving the ball again. If he can sink his shot out of the sand, he will have a six.

He misses.

1:25 P.M.

On the tenth hole, Grier Jones booms his drive off the tee, putting himself in perfect position for a second shot to the green. Gene Sarazen looks at Jones. "If you hit them all that way," he says, "you'll be all right."

Jones ducks his head and smiles.

2 P.M.

One of the veteran golf professionals—a Southerner, like the majority of pros—is eating lunch in the Augusta clubhouse. "A colored man couldn't sit down here and eat with me," he says, cynically, "but all the waiters and cooks are colored. I don't understand that. If I didn't trust a man, I'd rather have him eating across from me, where I can keep an eye on him, than in the kitchen, where he can tamper with my food."

THE MASTERS

The golfer's cynicism is based on the fact that no black golfer has ever been invited to play in the Masters. The people who run the Masters point out that no black golfer has ever qualified—under the various qualifying rules—and insist that, when one does, he will receive an invitation.

2:10 P.M.

Gene Littler finishes his practice round and, unhappy with his game, returns to the practice tee, trying to get his swing grooved once more. The tee is crowded with big-name players: Littler, Bob Goalby, Dan Sikes and Julius Boros.

"This is how you can tell it's a big tournament," says Boros. "Monday's usually a day off, but today everybody's out here looking for it."

Boros himself is experimenting. Joe Wolfe of the Wilson Sporting Goods Company stands next to him, studying his swing. "You're rushing," Wolfe says. "You're hurting your tempo."

Boros nods, slows down his swing, giving himself time to work his legs on the downswing, and makes cleaner contact. "I've got rhythm," hums Boros, who is fifty years old.

2:20 P.M.

As they walk up to the fifteenth hole, Herman Keiser turns to Grier Jones and says, "They've moved the tee back here."

Gene Sarazen stares down the fairway. "It's a little long now," he says.

On the final day of the 1935 Masters, Craig Wood birdied two of the last four holes and came in at 282, six under par, almost certain of winning the title that had escaped him by a single stroke the year before.

He held a commanding lead over the only man who could catch him: Gene Sarazen was three-under with four holes to go. On the par-five fifteenth hole, then playing at 485 yards, Sarazen boomed out his drive 265 yards.

April 6, 1970

He picked a four-wood for his next shot and hit it perfectly. The ball landed on the apron of the green, bounced up and rolled straight into the cup for a double-eagle deuce. It was the most spectacular shot in the history of golf.

Sarazen parred the next three holes, finished at six-under, and the next day, in a thirty-six hole playoff, beat Craig Wood by five strokes.

2:23 P.M.

Arnold Palmer's jet touches down at Daniel Field, the Augusta airport for private planes. Palmer himself piloted the jet from Greensboro to Latrobe yesterday, but today he let his regular pilot, Darrell Brown, handle the controls.

The first time Palmer played in the Masters, fifteen years ago, he arrived, with his wife, Winnie, in a trailer.

2:25 P.M.

Gene Sarazen marches down the fifteenth fairway to his drive, more than 220 yards off the tee. Two huge mounds, newly built, guard the right side of the fairway some thirty or forty yards closer to the green. The mounds look as if elephants were buried under them.

"Two large and several small mounds have been constructed on the right side of the fifteenth fairway," the Masters tournament committee has announced. "The players will now need to place their tee shots within a thirty-yard-wide area, between the two pines (on the left) and the mounds, in order to have a clear shot at the green. . . . The new location of the tee, plus the mounds, will make it necessary for the players to hit a straight drive or preferably one with a slight fade in order to place it in position for an open shot at the green. Without the advantage of the extra driving distance attainable in the past, the contestants will be obliged to hit a longer second shot in order to carry the pond and reach the green."

"Gonna get a double-eagle today, Gene?" a spectator yells. Sarazen beams, at the memory, and takes a six.

2:30 P.M.

Shot after shot, Bob Goalby wildly hooks his ball off the practice tee. Since he won the Masters in 1968, he has accomplished almost nothing. "Take a look at my swing," he says to Julius Boros.

Boros studies Goalby's swing.

"Turn instead of swaying as you go back," Boros says, "and you'll add ten yards."

"Turn what?" says Goalby. "Hips? Shoulders? What?"

"Turn everything," says Boros, "and then work your right shoulder in under the shot."

Goalby notices a reporter standing close to him and taking notes on the conversation. He launches a profane tirade against the eavesdropper.

As Goalby turns away, another player walks up to the reporter. "When he's like that," the player says, "the only thing to do is stay away from him. We're all under a little pressure this week, and some of us have trouble handling it."

2:50 P.M

On the twelfth hole, Gary Player, playing with Dale Douglass, Bunky Henry, Dean Refram and assorted plainclothesmen, hits his tee shot fifteen feet short of the pin and two-putts for a par.

Then he walks to the trap behind the right side of the green and places a ball under the lip. "Here's where I did it from, three years ago," says Player. "Blasted it in for a deuce. Greatest shot I ever made."

2:55 P.M.

Walking down the eighteenth fairway, Gene Sarazen turns to Herman Keiser. "The fellows today play too much golf," Sarazen says. "They burn themselves out."

April 6, 1970

"Yeah," Keiser says, "but they're millionaires by the time they're thirty-nine."

"And on their tombstones," Sarazen adds, "it says, 'Here lies a millionaire. The downhill putts got him.'"

3:05 P.M.

Larry Ziegler, a strong young pro making his Masters debut, comes off the eighteenth green after his first practice round. "How'd you like it?" a newspaperman asks him.

"Easy course, easy putting," Ziegler says, with a smile. Ziegler, who does his best putting with his driver, three-putted half a dozen holes.

3:10 P.M.

In the clubhouse following his round with Sarazen and Keiser, Grier Jones relaxes with his wife. "Janie," he says, "do you know the address of the place we've rented?"

"No, Grier," she says.

"I can't find the address or the telephone number," he says. "What'll we do?"

"I'll call my father back home," says Grier. "I left the address and phone number with him."

Jones calls his father in Wichita to find out where he's living in Augusta.

3:15 P.M.

After a long session on the practice tee, Julius Boros walks to the first tee to try out the course. He glances toward the green, takes out his driver and hits the ball down the right side of the fairway, the proper route to approach the green.

The ball lands in the fairway bunker.

Boros looks a little startled. Then he remembers that the bunker, which could be carried in the past by a drive of around 230 yards, has been moved back fifteen yards this year.

3:30 P.M.

The only man ever to lose the Masters on arithmetic, Roberto de Vicenzo, strolls into the lower locker room of the Augusta clubhouse, the gathering place for the players and the press. "You going out to practice, Roberto?" someone calls.

"Not me," says de Vicenzo. "I go to register, then I go home and rest."

The big Argentine smiles and puts his hand over his heart. "Must take these things easy," says de Vicenzo, who will be forty-seven next week. "Is no good for man my age to get to work too fast."

3:45 P.M.

A small division of newspapermen surrounds Billy Casper in the clubhouse. He is defending his conservative approach to the Augusta course. In 1969, he made a conscious decision not to attack the par-fives, to lay his second shots up short of the hazards, then wedge up and try to get his third shots close enough for putts at birdies.

"You can't attack this course," Casper says, "because of the pin placements. The way the greens get dried out, it's hard to hold your shots on them."

"What do you think of the mounds on fifteen?" someone asks.

"I guess I'll have more company laying up short of the pond," says Casper. "They make the hole more difficult. I'll need the wind behind me and nothing more than a four-wood before I'll go for that green now."

"What about moving back the bunker on the first hole?"

"The course is playing a stroke harder for me now," says Casper.

3:55 P.M.

Bert Yancey leaves the clubhouse and heads for his home in Augusta, the same place he stays each year, a house owned by

April 6, 1970

Mr. and Mrs. J. B. *Masters*. The Masters have set up a small trophy room for Yancey, filled with clippings and memorabilia of the Masters tournament and of Yancey's part in it. Mrs. Masters has even made a miniature green jacket that hangs in the trophy room.

On his right wrist, Yancey is wearing a copper bracelet—a voodoo bracelet. He has been troubled in the past by a sore elbow, and he feels that the copper bracelet, for some reason, extracts the acids from his body and the pain from his elbow. "It can't be just psychological," Yancey says. "They use the bracelets on horses in England, and it works."

Yancey is hurrying back to the Masters house to study his charts of the Augusta course, to reassess his strategy. He is deep in his Masters fog now.

4 P.M.

The amateur hope in the Masters, big Steve Melnyk, stands on the veranda outside the clubhouse, talking easily about a variety of subjects. He is a likable young man, both candid and cheerful.

First, he talks about the course. "There are more holes that are difficult than I had heard," he says. "Ten, eleven and twelve, for example. Five and seven. But it's easy to make a lot of birdies. If you can par ten, eleven and twelve, you can shoot the lights out on the back side."

Melnyk turns to the tournament in general. "Everything here has a little more class than any other tournament I've been around," he says. "Anywhere else you'd get a courtesy car, but the gas tank would be almost empty. Here you get a courtesy car, and the tank's full of gas. And everyone goes out of his way to make the amateurs feel special. That's one reason the tournament here is distinctive—the varied field, the amateurs and foreigners as well as the touring pros. The pros complain about the ratio, and I resent that. They play forty tournaments a year and all of them look alike. They can't stand to see one tournament that's different and appealing in a broader way. I'm surprised that a lot of the pros don't seem more intelligent than they do about anything other than golf."

Melnyk lumbers off, dragging his 240 pounds and his opinions with him.

4:15 P.M.

On the practice tee, Billy Casper picks up his driver and begins firing cannon shots down the range. "I'm getting an extra twenty to thirty yards out of the driver," he says. "I've been trying new sets of clubs periodically, but this is the first set I've gotten that feels good to me, that I want to keep using."

Casper's drives are not only long: They are hooking slightly, a distinct edge on the Augusta course. "I used to be a fader," Casper says, "and that hurt me here. It made the course play even longer. It feels good to have a driver I can draw the ball with."

4:10 P.M.

Even in the pro shop, Gary Player is flanked by a group of special guards. "You're really playing well," says a reporter.

"I'm playing *quite* well," says Player. *"Under the circumstances."*

4:40 P.M.

The Long Island Pro-Am champion, Jimmy Wright, sits in the clubhouse, sharing lunch with his wife, Joyce. "I'm getting a little tired," Wright says. "I played twenty-seven holes today, and maybe I'm over-golfed. My edge is gone."

Wright manages a smile. "I'm a little scared, too," he says. "Dave Marr told me he felt the same way the first time he came here. He said he got the feeling that if he didn't play well that week, he wouldn't go to heaven."

5 P.M.

Colonel Homer Shields, a retired Army officer who helps Clifford Roberts, a New York investment banker, run the

April 6, 1970

Masters, sits behind his desk in the tournament headquarters building. "We lost five days to rain last week," he says, shaking his head. "We're still putting up scoreboards. That should have been done long ago."

"What's the weather forecast for the rest of this week?" someone asks Shields.

"I never check," says Shields. "And I don't walk under ladders or in front of black cats, either."

5:05 P.M.

Dan Sikes—the Florida Sikes—walks on the practice green and sees that there are only two other men working on their putting—George Archer and Dale Douglass, both notoriously good putters. "Damn," says Sikes. "Look at them. They never stop. That's like Caruso practicing singing all the time."

5:15 P.M.

In the clubhouse, Tommy Aaron lounges in front of his locker, looking a little tired. Yesterday he played thirty-six holes with Palmer and Player, in front of a huge gallery. The crowds at Greensboro have earned a reputation of being the wildest and drunkest anywhere on the pro tour.

"They ought to strike a special medal for you," says Dave Hill, "just for finishing."

6:10 P.M.

Clifford Roberts, the chairman of the Masters tournament committee since the beginning, is sitting in the club's barber shop, getting a manicure and haircut. Sam Snead bursts in, grinning broadly and carrying a small-mouthed bass weighing more than eight pounds. Snead caught the fish a few minutes ago in Eisenhower Pond, behind the tenth fairway.

"Look at that!" Snead says. "Look at that!"

"That's a great catch," says Roberts. "Biggest of its kind I've seen here. Boros and the boys will have their work cut out for them."

Snead beams.

"Sam," says Roberts, "I don't believe you were this happy the first time you won the Masters."

7:15 P.M.

There are three ceremonial dinners for the players at the Masters each year—one for the foreign entries, one for the past champions and one for the amateur entries. The first 1970 dinner, for the foreign players, is about to begin in the lower locker room of the clubhouse. Colonel Homer Shields turns to the official Masters photographer, Frank Christian, who is setting up his lighting for the official dinner photo. "You sure you have enough lights?" says Shields.

"I have enough to light up Carnegie Hall," says Christian.

"I don't care about Carnegie Hall," says Shields. "Just the lower locker room."

Then Shields roams around the dining-room table and checks the seating arrangements. He sees that he has been placed next to Sukree Onsham from Bangkok. "This won't do," says Shields. "Better put me next to Kono. I speak better Japanese than Thai."

7:45 P.M.

At a private home rented by *Sports Illustrated*, members of the magazine's staff are entertaining friends and advertisers and potential advertisers. Many companies take homes in Augusta during the Masters and use the occasion to wine and dine customers and introduce them to professional golfers.

Dave Stockton and Bob Lunn, a pair of California pros, are the featured attractions at the *Sports Illustrated* party, and Stockton, an addicted fisherman, is giving an eyewitness report of Sam Snead's big bass catch. "Sam was fishing fast through the water," Stockton says, "throwing out his line sideways from the bank and then quickly bringing it across. That's difficult to do. Watching a guy catch one like that is like watching him run in a sixty-foot putt. It really puts pressure on you. You know you can't top a catch like Sam's, and you start worrying about getting anything at all."

The visiting businessmen soak up Stockton's fish story—and gin and vodka and scotch and bourbon.

9:45 P.M.

The Amvet Club is barely a mile from the Augusta National Golf Club, but the glamor of the Masters seems worlds away. A single long fluorescent light over the bar illuminates a large, stark room. A series of booths with red-plastic-covered seats faces the bar. Several of the seats are ripped as if they have been slashed. It is noisy, and a faded sign hangs over the door leading from the bar to a dance floor in back: POSITIVELY NO WEAPONS ALLOWED. EVERYONE WILL BE SEARCHED ON THE DANCE FLOOR.

This is where the caddies who work the Masters stage their own ceremonial dinners. The main course is a pint of Budweiser at forty cents. Roughly a third of the men in the room are wearing caddy hats, in Masters green, of course.

Howard Foote sits on a stool near the front door. He is a caddy at the Atlanta Country Club, but he came to Augusta by Greyhound bus yesterday and now he is staying at the Red Star Hotel. His room, shared with another caddy, is costing him fifteen dollars for the week. He is caddying in the Masters for Harold Henning, a South African. "Doesn't bother me," says Foote. "I'm not prejudiced."

Andrew Bradley, another caddy from Atlanta, sits near Foote at the bar. He has been up since 5:45 in the morning, even though, after a long night at the Amvet, he didn't get to sleep till 4:30. "I feel like an animal when I caddy a tournament," Bradley says. "Time is automatic. There's no problem waking up."

Bradley has been assigned the bag of John Bohmann, a young Texas amateur playing in his second Masters. Bohmann is not exactly among the favorites at Augusta National. Last year,

Bohmann shot 77-82—the second highest score of everyone entered—and missed the cut by eleven strokes.

"He doesn't do anything great," Bradley concedes, "but he does a lot of things good."

"You ain't gonna make much money with him," someone says.

"I'm not here for the money," Bradley says. "If I just wanted money, I could have stayed home and worked."

Bradley sips at his pint of Bud. "I'm here to caddy in the world's greatest golf tournament," he says.

TUESDAY

April 7, 1970

The Fairways Grow Narrower

F*or the second straight year, and only the second time in the history of the Masters, Bobby Jones is missing from Augusta. Sixty-eight years old now, partially paralyzed by a crippling disease similar to arthritis, Jones weighs less than one hundred pounds. But still, confined to a wheelchair, he occasionally travels to his Atlanta office at the law firm of Bird, Jones and Howell, and he always follows the progress of the Masters. The tournament, incidentally, was originally called the Augusta National Invitation, and no one knows for certain who dreamed up the name "Masters." "I must admit," Bobby Jones has said, "that the name was rather born of immodesty."*

Although he is more than one hundred miles away, Jones' influence permeates Augusta. He once offered a classic definition of the pressure of a major tournament—"One always feels that he is running from something without knowing what nor where it is"—and now, only two days before the Masters is to begin, the golfers are running.

As the pressure swells, it is heaviest upon the cluster of favorites, the four men given the best chance to win: Jack Nicklaus, Gary Player, Bert Yancey and Billy Casper. Right behind them comes a whole flock of golfers, including Arnold

Palmer and Tony Jacklin and Bruce Devlin and Ray Floyd and Miller Barber and Dave Hill and Tommy Aaron and Tom Weiskopf and Frank Beard, and all of them, too, can taste the pressure. So can Steve Melnyk, trying to uphold the amateurs, and so can Sukree Onsham, the first Thai ever to play at Augusta.

The tension of the Masters has a habit of crushing men: In 1936, in the opening round, Craig Wood—who had finished second in each of the first two Masters, who had opened with a 71 in 1934 and a 69 in 1935—shot an almost unbelievable 88. The next day, with no pressure on him, the same man playing the same course shot a 67.

In 1951, Sam Snead went into the final round tied for first place. Going back to 1946, Snead had played twenty-three straight rounds in the Masters with no score worse than 75. But then he shot an 80 and lost the Masters by eleven strokes. Ben Hogan won.

The following year, Hogan went into the final round tied for first place. Going back to 1939, Hogan had played thirty-nine straight rounds in the Masters with no score worse than 77, with twenty-three of those rounds under 72. But then he shot a 79 and lost the Masters by seven strokes. Sam Snead won.

Obviously, no one is immune to Masters pressure. "Every day, every minute," says Frank Beard, explaining the psychological impact of the Masters, "the greens get a little more difficult to read, and the fairways grow narrower."

8:10 A.M.

Two American amateurs—Dick Siderowf, a thirty-two-year-old stockbroker from Connecticut, and Ed Updegraff, a forty-eight-year-old urologist from Arizona—are eating breakfast in the lower locker room. Siderowf picks up a newspaper and flips quickly to the stock tables. "I can't help thinking that

April 7, 1970

the medical-supply companies have to be good in the long run," the broker tells the doctor.

Siderowf scans the list and adds, "American Hospital was up an eighth yesterday."

Another amateur, John Farquhar, a Texan, joins Siderowf and Updegraff. Farquhar makes the score Wall Street 2, Medicine 1.

8:45 A.M.

Bert Yancey and Bruce Devlin are arguing, over breakfast, as to which is the weaker driver. "I wish I had your strength, Bert," says Devlin.

"Oh, c'mon," says Yancey. "You outdrive me by thirty yards."

"I don't think either of us is going to win any prizes for distance here," says Devlin.

They start discussing the toughened first and fifteenth holes, and they agree that the changes will benefit the real big hitters—Jack Nicklaus, Tom Weiskopf, Ray Floyd—who can carry the new bunker on one and overcome the mounds on fifteen, and the real light hitters—Deane Beman is the prime example—who can't reach either the bunker or the mounds.

"That bunker on one used to be scary," says Yancey, "but now it's downright petrifying."

Devlin nods.

"And you've got no choice," Yancey says. "You've got to play the hole the short way, down the right. Who wants to play it safe to the left?"

"I do," says Devlin.

8:50 A.M.

On the first tee, William Hamilton, a civil engineer from Atlanta who works as a volunteer gallery guard during the Masters, shuffles through a stack of mimeographed sheets. The sheets, headed NOTICE TO CONTESTANTS, offer the following advice: "Only one ball is to be played in practice rounds, except two balls may be played from No. 1 and No. 15 tees. Your cooperation is expected and will be appreciated. RULES COMMITTEE."

9:15 A.M.

A twelve-year-old boy stands near the practice green, watching the players putt. He is wearing tan slacks and a white shirt with an alligator symbol. He is Robert T. Jones, IV, Bobby Jones' grandson, attending the Masters for the first time.

"Of course I'm excited," he says. "How can you not be excited? There are really such very fine players here."

A few Pinkerton guards walk by. There are one hundred and fifty of them working at the Masters, supplemented by city police, state police, FBI agents and members of the Richmond County riot squad. Some security men stay on duty all night, guarding the course and guarding the house where Gary Player is staying.

"It's a shame," says Robert T. Jones, IV, "that something like that might mar all of this."

He glances out over the course his grandfather built.

9:25 A.M.

Gene Littler and Phil Rodgers, a pair of Southern Californians who are sharing a house in Augusta, move to the first tee. William Hamilton, the gallery guard, hands them each a copy of the notice about the first and fifteenth tees. Littler reads the piece of paper, crumples it up and tosses it into a litter basket. Rodgers reads his copy, smiles and says, "I'll remember that."

Then Rodgers hits his tee shot down the middle of the fairway, steps back and cues the gallery to applaud.

Littler drives, also down the middle, and Rodgers again leads the gallery in cheers.

Neither man takes a second drive.

Littler and Rodgers together talk as much as any two normal people—and Littler says almost nothing.

April 7, 1970

9:35 A.M.

Deane Beman, who shot a 31 on the front nine during his practice round yesterday, sits in the clubhouse, eating breakfast and complaining of the pains in his back. "It's getting worse," he says. "I've tried a board on my bed. I've tried almost everything."

Beman groans. "I'm heading for the floor tonight," he says.

9:45 A.M.

On the putting green, in bright green slacks, Bert Yancey is explaining how he lost twenty pounds in the past four months. "There's no mystery," he says. "I just went on a diet—an anti-junk diet: No bread or candy. Listen, I'd starve to play golf."

9:50 A.M.

George Archer comes into the clubhouse and sits down in front of his locker, under a glass case holding mementos of the Masters donated by past champions—Jimmy Demaret's putter, Archer's own five-iron, the club he used to reach the eighteenth green during the final round a year ago. "I feel good," Archer says. "Maybe I'll get lucky and feel bad again."

When Archer arrived at the Masters last year, he was feeling miserable, suffering from intestinal flu. An opening 67 helped soothe his stomach.

"Are you treated differently this year, being the defending champion?" someone asks.

"Sure," says Archer. "Last year, nobody asked me for my opinions."

Archer walks to the rack in the locker room where the green jackets of the Masters champions are hung. The jackets do not leave Augusta; they are kept in the clubhouse to be worn each year only during Masters Week.

"Two months ago," Archer says, "the Masters people mailed me my green jacket to see if it fit. It was too small."

Archer, who is six-foot-six, wears a 42 extra-long. "I sent it back and told them how to fix it," he says. "Three weeks ago, I got a new jacket in the mail."

He points to the jacket on the rack. "This one fits," he says. "I'll wear it tonight to the Masters dinner."

10:05 A.M.

A movie cameraman is filming Sam Snead on the practice tee. Snead is hitting crisp iron shots. "What are you hitting?" the cameraman asks Snead.

Snead ignores the question.

The cameraman thinks Snead may not have heard him. "What are you hitting?" he asks again.

Snead ignores him.

Still, the cameraman wants to know which iron Snead is using. "What are you hitting?" he asks a third time.

Snead turns. "Wilson," he says.

10:10 A.M.

Dave Marr and Lionel Hebert are eating breakfast in the lower locker room, and Hebert is discussing his problems with his game. "I've got the yips," he says. "Not with my putter. With my wedge."

Mar nods sympathetically.

"You know," Hebert continues, "I shot 70-71-70-70 at Greensboro. The way I'm playing, I can do that on any course."

Hebert brightens. He is dreaming about winning the Masters in his fourteenth try.

10:15 A.M.

Gay Brewer and R.H. Sikes—the Arkansas Sikes, the quieter one—are sitting across the room from Marr and Hebert, and Brewer is talking about the importance of local knowledge at Augusta National. "More you play here," says Brewer, called Hound Dog for his drawl and his look, "more you know."

Sikes laughs. "I wouldn't know," he says. "I've never played here on Saturday or Sunday. Thursday and Friday local knowledge doesn't count."

The Arkansan is exaggerating, of course. In six previous ap-

Behind the Scenes: In the press building, a reporter can follow every hole of the Masters without ever touching a fairway. While the newsmen polish their prose, workmen polish the permanent trophy, a replica of the Augusta National clubhouse.

Galleryites: Among the tens of thousands of spectators who flock to the Masters, spilling onto the veranda and the fairways, a few stand out: Henry Picard, the 1938 Masters champion, wears a hat autographed by the contemporary stars; Frank Gifford leads, and Susan Marr, the wife of golfer Dave Marr, follows; a gentleman offers a lady a seat.

Arnold Palmer: The problem wasn't his driving

Tom Weiskopf: With wife and schnauzer

Dave Hill: Get there, ba

Frank Beard: Drop, ball!

Dave Stockton: Which way does it break?

Steve Melnyk, Grier Jones and Jack Nicklaus

Takaaki Kono: Eagle eye

Sam Snead: No autographs, please!

Gene Sarazen: Double-eagle

Fred McLeod and **Jock Hutchison:** Anybody got an old tee?

Chi Chi Rodriguez: He didn't expect his prayers to be answered so quickly

Gary Player: Over the water; between the Pinkertons; out of the sand; if the putt had fallen, there would've been a three-way playoff

The Masters Fog: Bert Yancey on the green; in the trophy room with Mr. and Mrs. Masters; looking over material for slacks with Tom Weiskopf; chatting with his wife; ignoring Frank Beard's backgammon game

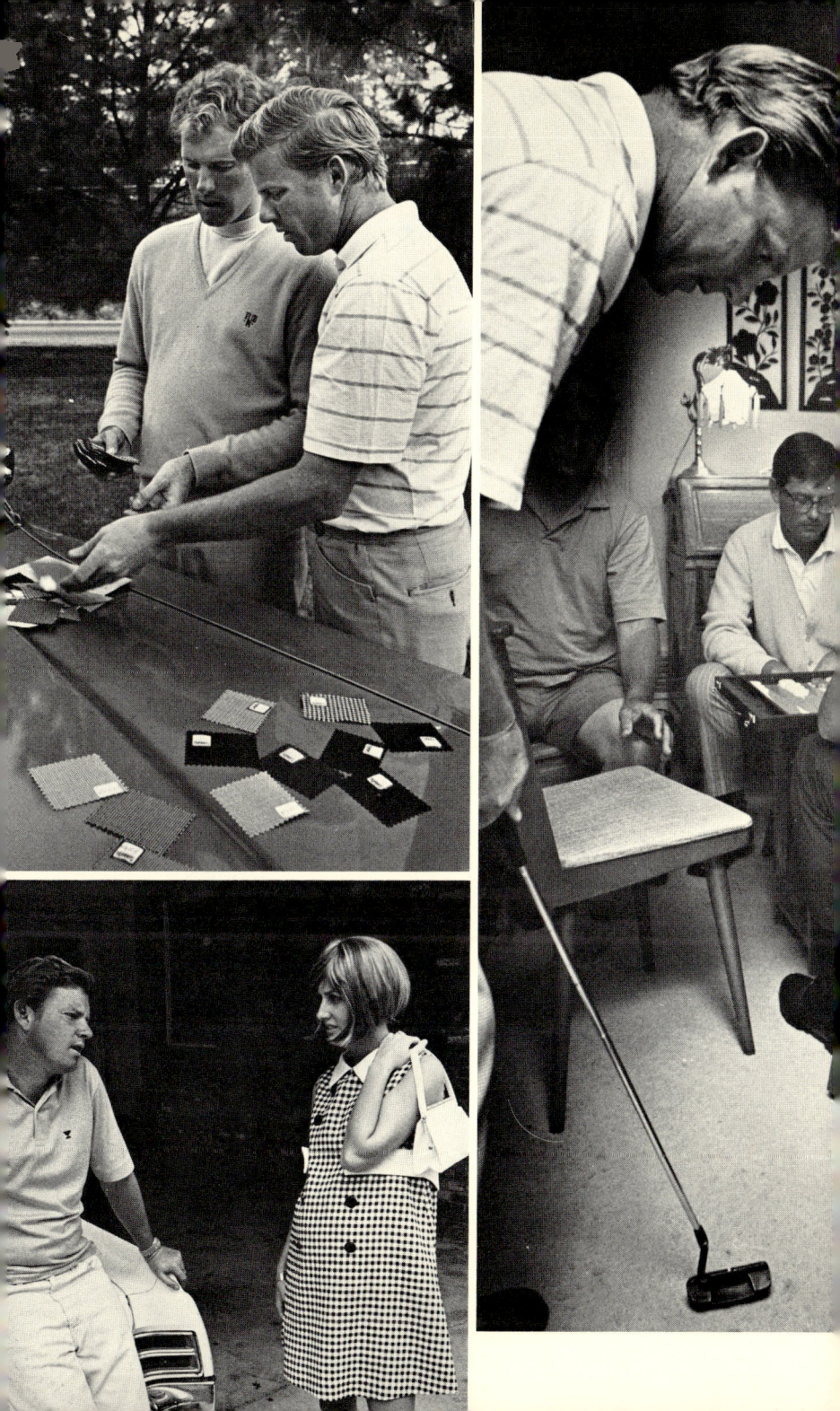

Gene the Machine: Gene Littler in a variety of moods, from reflective to ecstatic

Billy Casper: A little more body English, and the Masters would have ended a day so as George Archer said, "Casper to knees, Lord says no!"

The Caddies: On the course, advice f[or] Roberto de Vicenzo and interviews for t[he] press; off the course, beers at the Amvet Cl[ub]

April 7, 1970

pearances at the Masters, he has made the cut three times. But he has never made the top twenty-four.

"You gonna play a practice round today?" someone asks Sikes.

R.H. shakes his head. He is razor-thin. "I'm not strong enough," he says. "Maybe I'll play a round tomorrow, but probably not. I'll save my energy for Thursday."

10:25 A.M.

Steve Melnyk is working his way through a huge mound of practice balls on the driving range. "If I play in the morning," he says, "I have to hit a lot of balls to get loose. And I want to be loose this morning. We've got a big match going—Vinnie Giles and I against Dan Sikes and Dave Hill—the amateurs against the pros."

There is a glint in Melnyk's eyes. "I think we'll be OK," he says.

10:30 A.M.

The thinnest Jack Nicklaus Augusta has ever seen returns to the course. "I spent all day yesterday in Palm Beach," he tells a reporter. "I hit a few balls in the afternoon, then took my oldest son, Jackie, to Little League practice. I had to help out there. They made me work out the pitchers. I was afraid of hurting a finger, but then I figured, 'How hard can eight-year-old pitchers throw?'"

11:05 A.M.

Steve Melnyk has moved to the practice green, but he is not putting. He is standing off to the side, watching Arnold Palmer putt. In the early 1960s, when Melnyk was in his teens, he used to come up to Augusta to watch Palmer charge in the Masters.

11:10 A.M.

On the first tee, Gary Player takes his driver from his caddy. Player is not using the caddy originally assigned to him. The first caddy—who had carried Player's clubs for several years—asked to be reassigned, supposedly after threats from black militants in Augusta.

"I love everybody," says Player. "Regardless of religion or race."

11:15 A.M.

Vinnie Giles, playing in his third Masters, turns to Steve Melnyk on the putting green. "Notice the change?" Giles says.

"What's that?" says Melnyk.

"Arnie left the green and took his crowd with him," says Giles, "and the wind came up."

11:20 A.M.

Standing behind the ninth green, Mrs. Francis Stockton of Tallahassee, Florida, hears a huge roar. She turns toward the sound. "Palmer just teed off," someone says.

"God," says Mrs. Stockton. "I missed Arnie. I should be shot."

11:30 A.M.

Charlie Coody, a Texan who describes himself as "one of the plain Vanilla Janes" on the golf tour, comes to the sixteenth hole on his practice round.

Coody steps to the tee and looks over the water toward the green. He frowns, about as close as he likes to come to showing emotion, and pulls out a six-iron.

After sixty-nine holes of the 1969 Masters, coming off a birdie on the fifteenth hole, Charlie Coody was one stroke in front of everyone else. "Just three pars," he told himself, "on these last three holes, and you can win."

Coody's playing partner, George Knudson, went first on the sixteenth hole and pumped a four-iron well beyond the pin. Coody hesitated. He thought of hitting a hard six-iron or a

April 7, 1970

smooth five. He decided against risking a weak shot that might splash in the water guarding the green. He used a five-iron and hooked the ball off the green.

Coody took a bogey on sixteen, a bogey on seventeen and a bogey on eighteen and finished two strokes behind George Archer. "I had it won," Coody said afterward, "if I'd just gotten those three little pars."

11:45 A.M.

The war between the pros and the amateurs is off. Dave Hill teed off early, so Steve Melnyk, Vinnie Giles and Dan Sikes play a threesome. Melnyk is a little disappointed to lose the match, but happy to be playing with Sikes, who has offered to give him a few tips on the course.

12:05 P.M.

Tony Jacklin, the effervescent British Open champion, is lunching in the main clubhouse with his wife, Vivien. Jacklin and Player and Devlin are the leaders of the overseas delegation to the Masters, and even though some American pros feel too many unqualified foreigners compete at Augusta, the invaders do remarkably well. For the past seven years, at least five non-Americans a year have placed in the top twenty-four finishers.

Jacklin is Britain's greatest golf hero. His victory in the British Open last year was the first by a native since 1951, and it boosted golf interest in Great Britain the way Palmer boosted it in the United States more than a decade earlier. When Jacklin cracked up his 150-mile-an-hour Jensen last December, wrecking the car but escaping unharmed, one British newspaper editorialized: "While we appreciate that Tony's zest for life has much to do with his present success in golf, he must remember that his assets belong to the nation."

Jacklin is talking about his five-month-old son. "He's going to be a golfer," Jacklin says. "He's got a terrific grip already. He's got his own little clubs, and the walls of his nursery are covered with a hand-painted mural of all the Walt Disney characters playing golf."

12:23 P.M.

Jock Hutchison lines up a three-foot putt on the sixteenth green, strokes the ball and misses. He taps it in, then limps off the green. Jock Hutchison was born eighty-five years ago in St. Andrews, Scotland, the place where golf was born quite a few years earlier.

He won the PGA in 1920 and the British Open in 1921, and now, each year, he and Fred McLeod, eighty-seven, the 1908 U.S. Open champion, are the honorary starters in the Masters, the first twosome off the tee.

Hutchison turns to the small gallery following him. "I want you to know," he says, "this is the only tournament I never won. And that's because I was too old when they started it."

12:25 P.M.

"Fore!" someone shouts, and Jane Jones, the wife of Grier Jones, ducks as an errant tee shot on the eleventh hole flies toward her. The ball misses her by five feet. "Grier's always telling me to be careful," she says, "not to get too close."

12:26 P.M.

His private gallery follows Jock Hutchison from the sixteenth green to the seventeenth tee. "You know the difference between a Scotsman and a coconut?" Hutchison asks everyone.

"What?" someone shouts.

"You can get a drink out of a coconut," says Hutchison.

12:27 P.M.

On the veranda outside the clubhouse, Shirley Casper, Billy's wife, is explaining that her husband did not spend the month before the Masters brooding about the tournament. "He doesn't believe in getting too psyched up," she says.

April 7, 1970

12:28 P.M.

Before Jock Hutchison tees off on the seventeenth, he turns to the crowd. "You know how much a Scotsman can drink?" he says.

"How much?" a straight man replies.

"Any *given* amount," says Hutchison.

Then he bounces his drive eighty or ninety yards off the tee. "I used to kick it that far," he says, heading up the fairway, using his driver as a cane.

12:47 P.M.

A veteran foursome comes off the eighteenth green—Doug Ford, Jerry Barber, Sam Snead and, the kid of the quartet, thirty-eight-year-old Bob Goalby—and a teenager named Daniel Dukes greets each of them with his autograph book. Dukes is from St. George, South Carolina, eighty miles from Augusta.

Doug Ford signs the book.

Jerry Barber signs.

Bob Goalby signs.

Sam Snead stops and looks at the autograph book. "What's that?" says Snead, and without waiting for an answer, he marches past Daniel Dukes toward the clubhouse.

"I really wanted Snead's autograph, too," says the youngster.

1 P.M.

Grier Jones spots his wife walking along the side of the fourteenth fairway and hurries over to her. "I saw what happened back there at eleven," he says. "How many times did I tell you to be careful? I've got enough to worry about out here without having to worry about you."

1:05 P.M.

Homero Blancas, one of the two Mexican-American regulars on the pro golf tour, is on the putting green. "Hey, Homero," a spectator yells. "You miss Trevino?"

"Hell, no," says Blancas. "All I have to do is finish and I'll be low Mex."

1:10 P.M.

Gene Littler and Phil Rodgers finish their practice round, and a reporter walks up to them. "What did you do last night, Gene?" he asks.

"Just sat around with Phil talking golf," Littler says. "Grilled a couple of steaks and watched TV until bedtime."

"How'd you play today?"

"Still lousy," Littler admits.

"Think you can work it out?"

"Heck, yes," says Littler. "If I didn't, I'd take the clubs home and put 'em in the garage with my cars."

1:12 P.M.

Ray Floyd comes off the ninth green, having shot a 30 on the front nine of his practice round, a score that has never been matched in competition. The defending PGA champion, Floyd has to be considered a threat for the championship. Two years ago, he became the first man ever to shoot four straight sub-par rounds at Augusta without winning or tying for first: He didn't even make the top five.

1:18 P.M.

The phone rings in the Masters message center, and Kay Haun, a seventeen-year-old high school senior, answers. "Vice President Agnew is calling Arnold Palmer," a voice says.

Kay covers the mouthpiece and whispers to Sylvia Outlay, another high school senior, "It's the Vice President!"

She turns back to the phone. "Arnold Palmer's out on the course," she says.

"Is there any way you can reach him?"

"We're not allowed," says Kay. "We can only take the message, and if he stops by, we'll give it to him."

April 7, 1970

1:35 P.M.

Dave Hill and Howie Johnson are nearing the end of their practice round. Johnson is making his first appearance in the Masters at the age of forty-four. Last year, he earned $52,000 on the pro tour, the first time in his career he had earned more than $30,000.

As Hill goes to tee up his ball on the seventeenth hole, someone in the gallery shouts, "How 'bout a beer, Dave?"

The typical pro golfer would be offended by such a remark. Hill, a peppery young man, is not typical.

"Sure," he says, "why not? It's picnic country, isn't it?"

1:40 P.M.

Chi Chi Rodriguez, the Puerto Rican pro, moves from the seventh green to the eighth tee, and a spectator calls, "Gained a little weight, Chi Chi?"

"Yes, sir," says Rodriguez, "I'm on steak now. With $200,000 a year, ain't no sense in eating rice and beans any more."

The crowd laughs, and a little lady, holding a camera, turns to her husband and says, "Don't hear too many of them chattering like that."

1:55 P.M.

As Grier Jones comes off the eighteenth green, a swarm of teenaged girls descends on him, fluttering like butterflies in miniskirts, asking for his autograph. Jane Jones, as pert and miniskirted as any of the teenagers, scowls. "Boy," she says, "my husband has to have will power—and I have to have self-confidence."

2:17 P.M.

Chi Chi Rodriguez moves down the tenth fairway, and as he passes a cluster of fans along the ropes, he says to them, "Are you in Arnie's Army?"

"Arnie who?" somebody shouts.

"Arnie Rodriguez," says Chi Chi.

2:30 P.M.

Steve Melnyk's tee shot on the short twelfth hole carries to the fringe beyond the green. Melnyk chips his second shot and the ball rolls well beyond the hole.

Dan Sikes, the veteran pro, walks over to Melnyk. "You'll dance one right into the water that way," says Sikes. "You'll be better off always putting from up there."

Melnyk nods and thanks the pro for the advice.

2:35 P.M.

On the eleventh hole, Chi Chi Rodriguez powers a drive straight down the middle of the fairway, and someone in the crowd shouts, "Good drive, Chi Chi."

Rodriguez spins around. "I've been doing that all day," he says. "The last time I left the fairway was to answer the telephone. And it was a wrong number."

Chi Chi stops and delivers one of his monologues. "You know," he says, "some people say this is a rough life. I get up in the morning and come and play golf all day and make $200,000. That's hard work?"

He pauses. "Some people say golf pros are athletes," Chi Chi says. Then he points at his own thin 130-pound frame. "How the hell can you call me an athlete?" he demands.

2:50 P.M.

Roberto de Vicenzo, the easy-going Argentine, lumbers into the clubhouse. "How'd you do, Roberto?" a reporter asks.

"Just played the course to see if it is the same," de Vicenzo says. "It is, pretty much. How do I do? Some good, some bad. Is just exercise."

2:53 P.M.

Chi Chi Rodriguez moves down the thirteenth fairway, and as he passes a cluster of fans along the ropes—a new audience—he says to them, "Are you in Arnie's Army?"

"Arnie who?" somebody shouts.

"Arnie Rodriguez," says Chi Chi.

April 7, 1970

3:05 P.M.

"How'd you like to be paired with Player?" someone asks Gene Littler, who enjoys playing with a quiet gallery and few distractions.

"I haven't thought of that," says Littler. "It sure doesn't seem to be bothering Gary, does it?"

Littler thinks for a moment. "Maybe the best way to do it would be just to stay on the other side of the fairway," he says.

3:13 P.M.

Chi Chi Rodriguez is delayed at the fifteenth tee. Arnold Palmer is playing in front of him, and Arnie's Army is crossing the fairway. "Hey, Arnie," Rodriguez shouts, "how 'bout letting us play through?"

Then he turns to the crowd and says, "Now we'll have to wait for Arnie's caddy to fly over."

3:15 P.M.

Julius Boros prowls the locker room, grumbling about the bass Sam Snead caught yesterday. Boros is unhappy for two reasons:

1. Everyone is saying Snead's catch is the biggest in Masters history. "I caught a bigger one last year," Boros insists.
2. Too many people know about Snead's catch. "Everyone's out at the pond now," Boros says. "A bunch of amateurs."

Boros seems more concerned about his fishing than about his golf game, which has been in a decline for the past year. "I wish they'd put in a senior division here," says Boros, who turned fifty last month.

3:17 P.M.

Rodriguez hits a long drive off the fifteenth tee. "How do you hit the ball so far?" a spectator asks.

"Rice and beans," says Chi Chi. "Puerto Rican power."

As he strides up the fairway, Rodriguez walks over to the ropes and begins chatting with the gallery again. "Hey," he says,

"I think you people ought to say something about walking outside the ropes while a Puerto Rican walks on the inside."

3:30 P.M.

After his practice round, Gary Player sits in the locker room and talks about his ambition in golf. He is one of four players—Gene Sarazen, Ben Hogan and Jack Nicklaus are the others—to have won the U.S. Open, the British Open, the Masters and the PGA. "My goal is to be the first to win them all a second time," he says. "That would be quite an achievement, don't you think?"

Player has already won the British Open twice. Three titles to go.

3:35 P.M.

"Hey, Chi Chi," a spectator calls, "are you a rum head?"

"You know what I did here one year?" Rodriguez says. "I was so nervous I drank a fifth of rum before I played."

"What happened?"

"I shot the happiest 83 of my life."

3:40 P.M.

Jack Nicklaus comes off the course with a 70 for his practice round. "My swing's in good position now," he says.

"How do you like the course?" someone asks.

"The grass is sparse and the greens are fast," Nicklaus says. "The course is playing the way I like it. If I play well, I'll score well."

"How'd you do on fifteen?"

"I had between a one-iron and a three-wood to the green," Nicklaus says. "I used the three-wood because I was behind a mound. I choked down on it, but hit the ball too high on the club and just barely carried over the water. I two-putted for my birdie."

Everyone else is moaning about not being able to shoot for

April 7, 1970

the fifteenth green, and Nicklaus misses his shot and reaches the green.

"Have you reached your peak yet?"

"No," Nicklaus says. "I hope I reach it sometime between Thursday and Sunday."

3:53 P.M.

On the practice range, Billy Casper is pounding out 270-yard drives. "I'm in love with these new clubs," he says. "I can win this thing with a little good fortune."

4:05 P.M.

Bob Rosburg is sitting in front of his locker. He has played in fifteen Masters tournaments, but last year, for the first time in a decade, he failed to qualify. Like all former PGA champions (and all former U.S. and British Open and U.S. and British Amateur champions), he was invited to the tournament as an honorary, non-competing participant.

"I came," says Rosburg, one of the most personable and candid of the touring pros, "but I didn't have any fun. I missed playing."

Last June, Rosburg tied for second in the U.S. Open and qualified to play in the 1970 Masters. "It sure beats gallerying," says Rosburg.

4:07 P.M.

As Rodriguez comes off the eighteenth green, a fan shouts, "How'd you do?"

"Four-under," says Chi Chi.

"Wow!"

"I skipped two holes," says Chi Chi.

4:15 P.M.

Outside the locker room, on the porch facing the first tee, Arnold Palmer is being interviewed. Regally, the king of Augusta offers a few predictable platitudes about the beauty of the course.

the heritage of the tournament and his own hopes for having a good week. He sounds a bit like his friend, Spiro T. Agnew, listing the virtues of Richard Nixon.

Palmer's comments on the fifteenth hole are mild. "The mounds are fine," he says. "They make it a better hole. It'll sure as hell help Jack, but I'm not sure it'll help me. I hit two real good shots today, a driver and a three-wood, both as hard as I could hit them, and I just barely got on. Actually, I was a foot short of the putting surface. If it had been the tournament today, I probably wouldn't even have gone for it."

Then Palmer dismisses his audience and goes to call the Vice President.

4:18 P.M.

In the upstairs bar, for men only, Steve Melnyk is drinking beers and putting them on Dan Sikes' tab. Melnyk shot a 71, but Sikes beat him by chipping in on the eighteenth hole. "I think we've played together eight times," Sikes says, "and I've birdied the last hole seven times."

"Couple more rounds of beers," Melnyk says, "and I'll have my money back."

"Good match?" a reporter asks Sikes.

"I'll tell you," says Sikes, "I've often thought about getting into the agent business, managing athletes. If this guy turns pro, that'll make up my mind. I want a piece of his action. He sure as hell ought to get out of the life insurance business. He's the only shy life insurance salesman I ever saw. A guy says hello and he grins and ducks. He'd better turn pro."

Melnyk grins and ducks his head.

"Let me tell you about Steve on the second hole," says Sikes. "He hooked his drive into the dogwoods, and he went in there to play his second shot and you could barely see him. He looked like a guy peeking through a hedge at a nudist colony. He started taking these abbreviated practice swings to see if he had room to take the club back, and every time he drew it back he slapped the branches, and the most beautiful shower of flower petals would

April 7, 1970

come floating gently down. The sun was behind him, filtering through the trees, and it was a reverent scene. It was cathedral-like, I'll tell you."

Sikes nods. "Yeah," he says. "Steve chipped it out to the fairway."

4:35 P.M.

Two University of Southern California graduates, Al Geiberger and Dave Stockton, are sitting in the locker room. Stockton, one of the fishing set, is about to go to the pond. "You can always tell a golf pro fishing," says Geiberger. "He's wearing loud slacks, an alpaca sweater and alligator shoes."

Geiberger pauses. "Except Dave," he says. "He's wearing Levis, a T-shirt and alligator shoes."

4:45 P.M.

"The greens make this place tough," Jimmy Wright, the club pro, tells a reporter in the locker room. "It's not too difficult getting the ball to the greens, but their size, speed and contour can tear you up. I played with Herman Keiser today, and he said the greens were faster than he'd ever seen them, even on a Sunday."

Across the locker room, Dave Stockton offers a similar opinion. "These greens are frightening," he says. "You hit the ball hard, and it'll roll off the green. Hit it easy, and it'll break too much. They're the fastest I've ever seen."

Stockton doesn't look too frightened. Actually, putting is his strength, and the faster the greens, the better his chances to win the Masters.

4:55 P.M.

Dan Sikes is still holding court in the upstairs bar. Again, the talk is of the hard, fast Augusta National greens. "Jimmy Demaret once told me that, in 1950, the last time he won here," Sikes says, "he chipped instead of putting on some greens so that he could stop the ball near the hole."

Sikes sips at a drink. "People don't realize," he says, "how great a player Jimmy was to win here three times. He was a super finesse player."

Someone mentions Ben Hogan, and Sikes says, "There's the only guy I ever saw who, when he was on the practice tee, other players would stop what they were doing to watch him."

5 P.M.

Dave Stockton arrives at the fishing pond, accompanied by his caddy, Robert, toting his golf clubs. A Masters rule states that a caddy cannot accompany a player anywhere without the clubs; Robert has to bring the clubs to the pond. Stockton gives Robert all the fish he catches.

Stockton hooks onto a big bass—close to the Snead size—but, while he's reeling it in, the line snaps, and the fish darts away. Stockton groans, and Robert groans louder. The caddy sees his dinner swimming away.

6:30 PM.

Steve Melnyk discovers that, in the opening round Thursday, he will be teeing off at 12:23. His playing partner will be Jack Nicklaus. "It's nice to play with someone who knows the course," says Melnyk.

7 P.M.

In the J. B. Masters house, only a few hundred yards from the Augusta National grounds, Bert Yancey is playing backgammon with Frank Beard. A few of Yancey's friends and family are around, drinking and laughing.

In the kitchen, there is a yellow light bulb, unlit. The bulb was installed at Yancey's request. When the light is on, the parties end in the Masters house. No one is to talk loudly. When the light is on, Bert Yancey is resting for the Masters.

8:25 P.M.

At the annual dinner of the Masters champions, a short, leathery man steals the spotlight from Palmer, from Nicklaus,

April 7, 1970

from Player, from everyone. He limps occasionally, and he is fifty-seven years old, but still Ben Hogan is the golfer's golfer.

Throughout his active career, Hogan was known as "The Ice Man," the most determined, the most single-minded golfer of all. But now he seems mellowed, warm and sentimental.

Hogan gets up to speak and talks about how much the Masters means to him and how much the dinner of champions means to him. He asks that each champion try to attend the dinner for the rest of his life.

And then Hogan, who flew into Augusta today, turns and leaves and takes off immediately for his home in Fort Worth. He has not changed completely. He will not even watch a tournament he does not think he can win.

WEDNESDAY

April 8, 1970

Tapering Off

In the last desperate hours before the championship begins, tickets for the Masters are scarcer than double-eagles. Augusta National does not disclose how many tickets are sold—the least expensive go for twenty dollars, providing general admission for all four days of competition—but estimates begin at 20,000 and range upward to more than 30,000. Still, they have been sold out for months, and even months ago, only people who knew somebody who knew somebody were able to purchase any.

Augusta is swelling far beyond its normal population of 68,000. Many of the residents have left town, renting out their homes to golfers or golf fans, and disappearing for a paid vacation at South Carolina's Hilton Head Island or in Florida or even way up north in Washington, D.C. Some homes go for $2,000 during Masters Week; the same homes rent for less than $400 a month the rest of the year.

The local stores are ready for booming business. The five-and-ten-cent store in the shopping plaza across the street from Augusta National is setting up tables in its aisles, to serve breakfasts and lunches, and Schwartz's Delicatessen, in the same shopping plaza, has imported from Atlanta hundreds of extra bagels.

The sleepy Southern town is beginning to vibrate.

The Masters

It is a quiet day for the golfers. The course closes at two o'clock; in the afternoon, Augusta National receives its final grooming. The greens are cut once more at nine-sixty-fourths of an inch, the fairways trimmed at three eighths of an inch.

Most of the contestants try to play nine holes in the morning, either the front nine or the back. Some pick the nine that has been troubling them, taking one last chance to puzzle it out. Others pick the nine that is easier for them, figuring they have one last chance to bolster their confidence.

The afternoon is reserved for the Masters' annual par-three contest—and for thinking about tomorrow.

6:30 A.M.

Vinnie Giles is up and dressed, walking toward the door of the room he and Steve Melnyk are sharing at Augusta National. Outside, the mowers are whirring, the birds singing. "Vinnie," Melnyk calls, from his bed, "you didn't get to sleep till two. What are you getting up so early for?"

"It's such a great golfing atmosphere," Giles says. "I don't want to miss any of it."

He walks out and stares at the eighteenth green, at the spot where the Masters championship is often decided.

9:35 A.M.

Billy Casper is on the putting green, and Curt Bushman hovers nearby, watching him possessively, like a man counting his money. Bushman is from UMI, Uni-Managers Incorporated, which, according to its brochure, guides the financial affairs of such athletes as Casper, Jerry West and Harmon Killebrew.

"I'll be doing business under that tree," says Bushman, nodding toward a great old water oak on the veranda. "That's where everyone operates here. Mostly, I'll just be side-stepping. Ed Barner, the president of our company, sets up the deals."

"What kind of endorsements does Casper have?" someone asks Bushman.

April 8, 1970

He mentions a life insurance company, a hair tonic, a golf-equipment company, a clothing manufacturer, a franchising operation.

"Is there anything you might consider inappropriate?"

"Oh, definitely," says Bushman.

"What have you turned down, for instance?"

"Nothing I can think of," says Bushman. "Except offers of too little money. Too little money is definitely inappropriate."

10:45 A.M.

On the seventh hole, Gary Player hooks his drive deep into the woods. He hits a second ball off the tee, then, instead of sending his caddy to retrieve the first shot, goes after it himself. Half a dozen Pinkertons pursue him into the woods. So does the gallery, thinking that Player is going to play the errant drive.

Player walks up to his ball, leans over, picks it up and stuffs it in his pocket.

"Nice out!" a spectator shouts.

Player laughs.

So do the Pinkertons, for the first time all week.

11:10 A.M.

In the final tune-up for the 1970 Masters, Frank Beard starts off par-eagle-birdie and permits himself a small smile. "I'd like to have saved those last two for tomorrow," he says.

11:15 A.M.

At a gathering of the Golf Writers Association of America, Clifford Roberts, the chairman of the Masters tournament committee, talks about Gary Player. "I remember the first time he came here," Roberts says. "It was in 1957, and we had only half a dozen or so foreign players in those days. I received a letter from Gary's dad telling me of his son's accomplishments in golf. Frankly, they weren't much. But it was an appealing letter, and Mr. Player went on to say that if Gary could get an invitation, he'd go out and pass the hat among his friends to pay Gary's way.

So, with Bob Jones' approval, I wrote back that Gary was in and start passing the hat. I recall that he played very capably."

A reporter asks Roberts about the protective setup at the Masters. "We are up to our elbows in security," Roberts says. "Gary Player has every right to expect the courtesy and respect of the American people. We feel we are prepared to assure it."

11:20 A.M.

As Dave Marr comes off the ninth green, heading for ten, a spectator walks up to him, carrying a camera. "Excuse me," he says hesitantly, "but may I take your picture?"

The spectator realizes that the majority of golfers are touchy about having their pictures taken during a round. Most golfers look upon cameras as their natural enemies, ready to click whenever they're ready to putt.

But Marr, who lives near New York City, recognizes the importance of good public relations. He won the PGA championship five years ago, but lately he has accomplished more on television, as a golf commentator, than on the course.

Marr flashes a big grin at the fan who has asked to take his picture. "I wish you would," he says.

11:25 A.M.

After both of them have holed out, Frank Beard and Larry Ziegler stand on the fourth green, practicing their putts from a variety of directions. "Nobody can read this green right," Beard tells Ziegler. "It looks like it oughta break that way, toward the tee, but it breaks the other, toward the road. I don't know why. I can't explain it. But it does."

11:30 A.M.

Clifford Roberts is explaining that Augusta National has no bitterness toward the missing man of the 1970 Masters, Lee Trevino. "We don't harbor any ill feelings," says Roberts. "If he is qualified—and I think he is—he certainly will receive an invitation next year. We're always disappointed when anyone who's invited can't be here."

April 8, 1970

Then Roberts neatly jabs a needle into Trevino. "He said he didn't think he could play this type of golf course," Roberts says. "Apparently, we have a better opinion of his game than he does. We think he is skillful enough to play any type of course."

11:40 A.M.

On the long thirteenth hole, Jimmy Wright hits a big drive, then powers a four-iron eight inches from the cup and taps in for an eagle. "I'm getting juiced up again," says Wright. "I'm anxious for it to start."

11:50 A.M.

"How'd you do this morning, Roberto?"

Roberto de Vicenzo smiles, mocking himself. "Hit some balls, play a little," he says. "I cannot work so hard like these boys today. Old fella must save himself for tomorrow, right?"

12:05 P.M.

Vinnie Giles is telling Steve Melnyk horror stories about the par-three tournament that will begin in about an hour. "Man," says Giles, "that first little ol' hole, just ninety yards long, looks about five feet wide with forty million people down both sides. Why, I remember one guy who stood there and cold-shanked one over onto the ninth green. About killed a whole bunch of fellas."

Melnyk grins. "Thanks a lot, pal," he says.

12:15 P.M.

The assistant pro at the Royal Bangkok Sports Club, Sukree Onsham, leans over a putt on the practice green. The Thai champion is twenty-six years old, stands five-foot-two and weighs 114 pounds. He looks like a two-iron.

But in the 1969 World Cup championship at Singapore, a tournament matching two-man teams from forty-five different nations, Sukree Onsham tied for third place in the individual competition, finishing only one stroke behind Roberto de Vicenzo and only two behind Lee Trevino. Because of Sukree's brilliant play, tiny Thailand tied for fourth in the team competition, beating out several nations with rich golfing traditions, including England, Australia, South Africa and Scotland.

On the edge of the green, Terry Clapp watches proudly as Sukree curls in his putt. Clapp is wearing a navy-blue blazer bearing the crest of the Royal Bangkok Sports Club. He is one of four American businessmen, living in Thailand, who first lobbied to get Sukree an invitation to the Masters and then conducted a campaign to raise funds to send Sukree to Augusta. The Committee for Thai Golf Abroad also needed money to send the head pro at the Royal Bangkok, a man named Chalaw, to Georgia—not to compete, but to keep Sukree company and to translate. Sukree's golf is considerably better than Chalaw's, but his English is worse. This is not necessarily a great compliment to Chalaw, because Sukree's English is almost non-existent.

Clapp is holding a copy of the fund-raising letter used by the Committee for Thai Golf Abroad. The letter begins:

Dear Sir,

Very few times in an individual's life does an opportunity occur whereby he can contribute to a better understanding between his country and to the world at large. To most of us the opportunity never comes. However, were the opportunity made available to us, certainly one could put his best effort to achieve the goal of a better understanding between nations. The role most of us play is that of a supporting actor without which the play cannot go on.

An opportunity to achieve this goal and to bring honor to himself and his country has been presented to Thailand's superb golfer, Sukree Onsham. The opportunity will occur on April 9th, 1970, at approximately 10 o'clock. At that time he will tee off at Augusta National Golf Course in Augusta, Georgia, participating in the Annual Masters Golf Championship. He will attempt to better such players as Arnold Palmer, Gary Player, Jack Nicklaus, and Billy Casper, and thereby win a green jacket and a place in Golf's Hall of Fame. Thousands of spectators will personally see him on the famed golf course and millions of television viewers will see him play the 12th through the 18th hole. Countless words of print will be written about him, which will be read avidly by millions in the States, Europe and Asia.

April 8, 1970

Just what will they see? They will see a 5 foot 2 inch Thai who weighs 114 lbs. who has a smile that would brighten up any golf tournament. They will also see a diminutive underdog hit his shots as far as the big boys and probably putt better. They will also see what they want; the reporters will see good copy; the small folks of the world will see their champion; the bigger folks will see a little guy hit the ball further than they could with two shots; the ladies will see a handsome Thai with a beautiful smile. In short, they will see a good example of the land in which we live, a pleasant, handsome man and a living example of the land of the "Smiling Thais."

They will also see one hell of a good golfer . . .

What are the chances of Sukree's winning the Master's Golf Championship? We realistically think they are slim, but nonetheless a chance exists . . .

"It was difficult to raise money," says Clapp's Thai wife, Kamala. "Thais are not very philanthropic. They can understand giving to an orphanage, but not to a golfer. Golf is not very important in Thailand. Most Thais never heard of the Masters."

Still, the committee raised $10,000—including $500 donations from Carroll Rosenbloom, the president of the Baltimore Colts, and James Linen, the president of Time Inc.—and now Sukree is only one day away from his attempt to win a green jacket and a place in Golf's Hall of Fame.

12:30 P.M.

Someone with a sense of humor has decided to introduce the defending Masters champion, George Archer, to the challenger from Thailand. They shake hands on the practice green, and Sukree Onsham stands on tiptoe and uses up all his English. "I wish you good luck," he says.

"Have a good tournament," the six-foot-six Archer calls down.

12:45 P.M.

Bert Yancey stands on the practice green, leaning on his putter. "My putting's coming along," he says. "That's the only part of my game that's been worrying me. I'm glad the greens are fast. Nobody's going to be making all the putts. The important thing is to get down in two from thirty feet without a lot of three-putts."

Yancey has his copper bracelet on one wrist—and a watch on the other. The watch band holds a metal insert with the calendar for April, 1970. The dates of the Masters tournament are circled in red.

12:50 P.M.

Larry Hinson is sitting in front of his locker, chatting with a reporter about a problem he has: He feels that too few people recognize him on the golf tour. A few other reporters wander by, but none of them stops to eavesdrop. Most of them don't recognize Hinson.

He is a tall, slim, twenty-four-year-old blond, a Georgian playing in his first Masters, who admits, frankly, in violation of the golfer's code, that he loves to play in front of galleries.

"I'd love to catch on with the people," he says. "I've spent a lot of time trying to think of a gimmick, a trademark, something to let them all know it's me."

Hinson talks about other golfers' trademarks: The late Tony Lema's practice of buying champagne for the press each time he won a tournament, Doug Sanders' spectacular wardrobe, Billy Casper's gamy diet, Lee Trevino's brashness, Chi Chi Rodriguez's wisecracks.

"I've got to get something that's me," Hinson says. "It can't be anybody else."

He has one idea—each time he holes out, he'll flip his ball to someone in the gallery—but he's not sure how well it would work. "I don't know what the golf-ball people would think about that," he says, "or, for that matter, what my playing partners might think. And if it got to be a scramble each time, it might bother my own concentration."

Hinson smiles. "With me," he says, "it just might have to

April 8, 1970

be colorful clothes. Just watch! If I'm still around Saturday and Sunday, I'm going to wear an outfit like you've never seen. Maybe plaid—head to toe."

1:05 P.M.

A reporter walks up to George Archer in the clubhouse and asks him if it's true that the Masters championship is worth a million dollars to the winner. Archer laughs. "Not for me," he says. "A million is a hundred thousand dollars ten times. I didn't make anything like that."

Archer shakes his head, brushing the million away. "The value is that it puts you in a very special class for the rest of your life. And you can't put a dollar sign on that."

1:15 P.M.

Steve Melnyk is eating lunch and looking forward to his first round in the Masters tomorrow. "I like the idea of playing with Nicklaus," he says. "Jack plays golf just the way I'd like to."

1:45 P.M.

Gene Littler and Phil Rodgers finish their nine-hole practice round, and a reporter walks up to them. "What did you do last night, Gene?" he asks.

"Just sat around with Phil talking golf," Littler says. "Grilled a couple of steaks and watched TV until bedtime."

"How'd you play today?"

"I still haven't found the answer," says Littler. "All I've done so far is get Phil fouled up, too."

1:48 P.M.

On the first hole of the par-three tournament, played on a picturesque course across the road from the Eisenhower Cottage, Steve Melnyk lines a wedge shot over the green, chips back up and takes a bogey four. "Can't complain," he says. "At least I didn't kill anybody."

The Masters

2:15 p.m.

Gene Littler steps up to the first tee on the par-three course. He smoothly strokes his shot, and the ball rolls into the cup for a hole-in-one.

"He's having a lot of trouble with his game," a reporter says.

2:30 p.m.

Julius Boros and Gene Sarazen have just completed the eighth hole in the par-three contest, and as they walk toward the ninth tee, Trent Long, a ten-year-old boy from Augusta, stops Sarazen and asks for his autograph. Trent hands Sarazen a sheet of paper and a pen.

Sarazen stares at the paper. "What's this on here?" he says. "Your arithmetic?"

"No, sir," says Trent. "That's Mr. Yung-Yo's autograph."

Hsieh Yung-Yo is Taiwan's delegate to the Masters.

3:05 p.m.

On the practice green, Chi Chi Rodriguez strokes a long putt. The ball rolls up toward the cup, hesitates and falls in. Chi Chi rushes up and covers the hole with his hat, and the small crowd around the green cheers, *"Ole!"*

Chi Chi's caddy, wearing No. 78, sits on the edge of the putting green, looking bored. "Same old stuff," he says.

The caddy is wearing the standard Masters outfit, white coveralls with green trim and a green caddy hat. Beneath the bland uniform, he is wearing brown slacks with a purple stripe and a pink-and-white sweater.

He glances at Rodriguez. "Corn, pure corn," he says, "but these chumps eat it up."

3:10 p.m.

Bruce Devlin stretches out in the locker room, resting his legs on a coffee table. "I'm a bit leg-weary," says Devlin, who underwent an operation for varicose veins a couple of years ago.

April 8, 1970

"I'm shin-sore, you might say. How will I be tomorrow? I never know how the legs will be till I roll out of bed in the morning."

3:25 P.M.

As Chi Chi Rodriguez lines up a putt on the practice green, J. F. Fannon, a scorer for the tournament, leans over the gallery rope and offers him a card. Chi Chi takes the card and reads it: "MY CARD, SIR. I AM A BULLTHROWER, BUT I RESPECT A PROFESSIONAL LIKE YOU. SO PLEASE CARRY ON."

3:35 P.M.

Harry the Horse, Harold Henning of South Africa, sprints through the par-three course in only 21 strokes, six birdies and three pars, the second lowest score in the history of the miniature Masters. "Nothing to it," he says. "I can use some of those putts tomorrow."

3:45 P.M.

Gene Littler is on the practice tee, hitting shot after shot, still looking for his game.

4:25 P.M.

In the Augusta National barbershop, Gary Player is getting his hair clipped. For once, he is not surrounded by Pinkertons. "I'm going to win it," Player tells the barber. "I'm fit."

11 P.M.

Dave Stockton, who has played forty-five practice holes in even par, sits in his rented home, in front of a television set. There is a program on, but Stockton barely notices it. His eyes are glazed, and he is deep in what he calls his "hate-developing process." He is trying to convince himself that everyone else in the tournament, and the golf course itself, are his enemies.

"It isn't easy," Stockton says, "because I'm a friendly guy. But if I don't do it, I have no chance to win."

THURSDAY

April 9, 1970

A Crystal Vase for the Bridesmaid

The eighty-five men who are teeing off today at Augusta National—eighty-three official competitors and two honorary starters—have a variety of goals. Perhaps half a dozen are thinking only about victory; anything less will disappoint them. This group includes Jack Nicklaus and Arnold Palmer and Gary Player, the multimillionaires of the sport; to them, second place means only more taxes to pay. It includes Billy Casper, the one millionaire who does not own a green Masters jacket. It definitely includes Bert Yancey, because of his obsession with winning the Masters, and it may include Tom Weiskopf, because he came so close last year.

Another two dozen players are thinking mostly about coming close. They do not discount the possibility of victory—they know that a George Archer or a Gay Brewer or a Bob Goalby can emerge from the pack—but they appreciate, realistically, how long the odds are against them. They will be proud to finish among the top five, pleased to be among the top ten. For the most part, they are the pros who regularly follow the tour, and their names range from Aaron to Ziegler, their nationalities from Australian to New Zealander. At least one amateur, Steve

Melnyk, falls in this category, along with at least one foreign pro who does not play the American tour, Takaaki Kono.

Possibly another two dozen players are thinking seriously about finishing among the top twenty-four, at best, and thus earning an automatic invitation to the 1971 Masters. They dream of coming close, of placing in the top ten, but they realize that their game does not quite justify such lofty hopes. They include young American pros, making their debuts at Augusta, and aging champions, their skills diminishing, and optimistic amateurs and foreigners. They know that every year there are surprises among the top twenty-four, always an amateur or a foreigner or a newcomer or a fading veteran who unexpectedly puts his game together and challenges the stars.

The remaining starters—untested amateurs, unheralded foreigners—have no hope greater than surviving the thirty-six-hole cut. And thirteen of the entries are more than forty-five years old, a majority of whom haven't a single thought of making the cut. They worry only about surviving eighteen holes at a time.

The goals range, obviously, from the modest to the magnificent, a perfect reflection of the talent assembled at Augusta.

1:10 A.M.

The terminal at Bush Airport is practically empty, only a handful of soldiers and Tony Jacklin. The British Open champion, who hopes to become the first Englishman ever to finish in the top twelve at Augusta, is waiting for his father to arrive from London. Jacklin will be teeing off in less than ten hours, and several of his friends offered to pick up his father for him, but Tony insisted upon going himself. His father taught him to play golf when he was eight years old, and now, seventeen years later, he is bringing his father to the United States to see how much he has learned.

April 9, 1970

6 A.M.

Jimmy Wright wakes up, exactly an hour before his alarm clock is supposed to ring, and begins to think about the drive he will hit on the first hole of his first Masters.

7:45 A.M.

A couple of dozen men, all of them black, are meeting behind the big scoreboard to the right of the first fairway. They are not militants, plotting the harassment of Gary Player. They are the forecaddies for the Masters, the men who, after a player hits a drive, run to where the ball winds up and stand there, holding a flag on the end of a long stick to mark the position. They are getting their final briefing. "Now, remember," one of the Masters officials tells the forecaddies, "hold your flag up straight."

8:20 A.M.

Room service has arrived in his comfortably spacious hotel room, and as Dan Sikes starts breakfast, he glances at the morning paper and sees an article that ruins his appetite. In the article, Gene Sarazen, commenting on the touring caddies who travel from tournament to tournament, implies that "these gypsy caddies" cheat, and urges they be banned. "They sign contracts with the players for a percentage of the winnings," Sarazen argues. "With this much money at stake, what is to prevent a caddy from moving a ball or teeing it up to improve his man's lie?"

Sikes has often tried to help the touring caddies—who are banned already from many summer tournaments, when teenagers replace them—improve their uncertain and nomadic existence. He goes out to the golf course furious.

8:45 A.M.

The crowd around the first tee is already ten-deep, watching a special ceremony for the traditional honorary starters, Fred McLeod and Jock Hutchison. Robert T. Jones, III, Bobby Jones' son, a Coca-Cola executive in Massachusetts, is presenting both octogenarians with trophies named after Frank Moran, a Scottish golf writer.

Gene Sarazen, wearing a checkered knickers suit, steps out of the clubhouse and looks down toward the first tee. Sam Snead walks by, and Sarazen, who is sixty-eight, yells to Snead, who is fifty-seven, "Hey, Sam! Don't you want to watch those old fellas tee off?"

8:55 A.M.

In the clubhouse, Dick Siderowf, the stockbroker from Connecticut, is explaining that when he got out of college a decade ago he found it much easier to remain an amateur than he would now. "The purses weren't nearly so large then," Siderowf says. "Now, if I were coming out of school, it'd be an awful temptation to turn pro. I don't see how you can pass up all that money."

9 A.M.

Fred McLeod, two years older than Jock Hutchison, has the honor, and he cracks his drive roughly 150 yards down the middle.

Hutchison steps up and turns to McLeod. "Can you lend me a tee?" he asks.

"What happened to the one I gave you last year?" says McLeod.

"How 'bout an old ball?" says Hutchison.

Then Hutchison smacks his drive down the middle, perhaps ten yards beyond McLeod's ball.

"Old Freddy moves off pretty good," says Dave Hill, standing behind the tee.

"Hope I'm doing that at seventy-five," says Gay Brewer.

Walt Bingham, a writer for *Sports Illustrated*, looks embarrassed. "They both outdrive me," Bingham admits.

As the two old champions march down the fairway, off to play a few ceremonial holes, one spectator stage-whispers, "Think they'll make the cut?"

"The cut?" another spectator responds. "They'll be lucky if they make the hill."

April 9, 1970

9:02 A.M.

In the dining room at the Alamo Plaza motel, Takaaki Kono sits down to a breakfast of scrambled eggs, bacon and coffee. If he were home in Japan, he would be eating *gyuniku no batayaki* (rice and seasoned meat and vegetables) for breakfast. "I was nervous last year," he says, "but not this year."

9:06 A.M.

Near the first tee, Dave Stockton, wearing a handsome raspberry shirt and gray slacks, walks over to a U.S. Army officer who is serving as official interpreter for Thailand's Sukree Onsham. Stockton is paired with Sukree and, to be polite, he wants to know how to say, "Good shot," in Thai.

"*Dii*," says the interpreter.

"How do you say, 'Very good shot'?" Stockton asks.

"*Dii mach*."

"Thanks," says Stockton.

9:07 A.M.

Dean Refram, a short, muscular pro from Florida, hits the first official shot of the 1970 Masters. He has no trouble with the bunker on the right side of the fairway: He hooks his drive off the fairway to the left. Then Larry Ziegler powers a big drive down the middle and strides off the tee with a smile on his face. He has passed the first hurdle.

9:14 A.M.

It is a dubious honor, but Dave Stockton is the first man in Masters history to put a drive in the new bunker on the opening hole. Stockton is one of the shorter drivers among the pros, and he seems more surprised by reaching the bunker than by landing in it.

His playing partner drives down the middle of the fairway, to the left and far short of the bunker. "*Dii*," says Dave Stockton.

Sukree Onsham smiles. Then he reaches the green with his second shot, and Stockton calls, "*Dii mach! Dii mach!*"

Sukree beams. But then Thailand's Little Tiger three-putts for a bogey. He turns to his interpreter and, through him, tells Stockton, "I am afraid we had better tell you how to say, 'Bad shot,' in my language."

9:41 A.M.

Jimmy Wright steps to the first tee. He has watched from the putting green as the previous two pairs teed off, and only one of the four golfers—Julius Boros—has put his drive in the fairway. "Jimmy," Wright tells himself, fighting off a slight case of butterflies, "you sure can't do any worse than those fellas, so go on and hit it."

He belts a long drive down the middle, then knocks his second shot nine feet from the pin. His first putt, not a bold one, stops short of the hole, and Wright taps in for his par. "I guess I might have really gone a little harder for that birdie," Wright says, "but I was figuring it's very important to start with a par."

9:49 A.M.

On the first hole, Grier Jones puts his tee shot into the fairway bunker. His father, W. R. "Tex" Jones, who is in the oil business and helps sponsor Grier on the tour, scowls. "He told me the one place he didn't want to put it was in the bunker," Tex Jones says. "Anywhere but there. Well, he's there, and here we go."

From the bunker, Grier Jones reaches the green with his second shot, then sinks a twenty-foot putt for a birdie. "That oughta pump him up pretty good," says his father, pumped up pretty good himself.

9:55 A.M.

On the veranda outside the clubhouse, two elderly members of Augusta National are chatting. "Who are you following today?" one of them asks.

April 9, 1970

"Melnyk," says the other.

He does not mention Steve Melnyk's playing partner, Jack Nicklaus.

At Augusta National, the amateurs still rule—at least on the veranda.

10:03 A.M.

Gene Littler waves his caddy in from the practice range. He is ready to move first to the putting green, then to the first tee. A reporter walks up to him. "What did you do last night, Gene?" he asks.

"Just sat around with Phil talking golf," Littler says. "Grilled a couple of steaks and watched TV until bedtime."

Littler manages a smile. "My nights aren't terribly exciting, are they?" he says.

10:10 A.M.

The tenth twosome of the day moves to the first tee, and the starter announces, "Juan Rodriguez." The skinny Puerto Rican in the white strawhat does a double-take. "Juan Rodriguez?" he says. "Who the hell is Juan?"

Then he turns to the gallery and, with a bow, introduces himself: "Better known as Chi Chi."

10:12 A.M.

As Gene Littler leaves the practice tee, Tommy Aaron comes on. Aaron looks at Littler admiringly. "Doesn't take a Rolls Royce long to warm up, does it?" says Aaron.

10:15 A.M.

Chi Chi Rodriguez's approach shot to the first green soars straight at the flag, actually lands in the cup on the fly, then bounces out and rolls twenty feet away. "The flags here are made of steel," Chi Chi says. "If they were made of fiber, like at other tournaments, the ball would've stayed in the cup. That's got to be the greatest shot of my life." Chi Chi is serious, for a change.

10:25 A.M.

Hsieh Yung-Yo of Nationalist China walks over to Frank Beard in the dining room and introduces himself. They will be teeing off together in an hour and a half. "You help me, all right?" says Hsieh Yung-Yo, in hesitant English.

Beard smiles. "You may have to help me," he says.

11:06 A.M.

On the first hole, Takaaki Kono's drive catches the bunker on the right side of the fairway. "He's very nervous," Midori Kono, his wife, says to Dr. Hiroshi Toyohara, a resident at a local hospital who is serving as interpreter for the Konos.

Dr. Toyohara turns to a bystander. "She is more nervous than he is," says the doctor.

11:10 A.M.

Frank Beard looks down the practice range. "I made up my mind last night," he says to a friend. "I'm going for it. I'm letting out the driver."

Beard kicks his practice balls. "It's not my style to gamble," he says, "but about four years ago, Mason Rudolph said to me, 'You know, Frank, if you're lucky, in your career, you get about thirty chances to win a major title—the Open or the Masters or the PGA. And when those chances come up, you've got to go after them. Those titles don't just come to you.' Well, for a long time, I didn't follow Mason's advice. I approached a big tournament just like I approached any other. But last night, I decided the hell with it. I've got to go for it."

11:12 A.M.

On the second hole, Gene Littler sinks an eight-foot putt for a birdie.

11:14 A.M.

The Little Tiger, Sukree Onsham, hits his approach shot to the right of the ninth green, some ten feet beyond the green-and-white gallery rope. A gallery guard loosens the rope and lets it fall to the ground.

April 9, 1970

Dave Stockton thoughtfully walks over to the guard and tells him to untie the rope and get it out of the way. Sukree, wearing turquoise slacks and shirt and pale-green socks, smiles gratefully at Stockton.

Then the tiny Thai takes a bogey to complete the front nine with a disastrous 42. "After he missed that short putt on the first hole," says Terry Clapp, who will have to explain Sukree's round to the rest of the Committee for Thai Golf Abroad, "he began to bogey all over the place."

Stockton, who has shot a 38 going out, has not had many opportunities to say, *"Dii mach."* Stockton himself is actually shaking from nervousness. "Jeez," he says, "I know this is the Masters, but this is ridiculous. I wasn't this nervous last year."

11:15 A.M.

Pro golf's rookie of the year in 1968, Bob Murphy, is paired with Grier Jones, the 1969 rookie of the year, and Murphy is suffering through a difficult round. On the sixth hole, he picks up his fourth bogey of the day. His wife, Gail, sighs, "I'm afraid he's going to shoot his weight," she says.

Murphy, who is in the watermelon business, is sometimes accused of concealing his products inside his shirt. He weighs 210 pounds.

11:30 A.M.

Mason Rudolph approaches the practice tee as Frank Beard is walking off. "Hey, Mase," Beard calls. "You were right four years ago."

"Huh?" says Rudolph.

"I'll tell you Sunday," says Beard, "when I see how it works out."

11:35 A.M.

As Chi Chi Rodriguez walks toward the seventh tee, someone in the gallery asks him how old he is. "I'm thirty-four," he says, "but a Puerto Rican thirty-four is like an American fifty."

11:50 A.M.

Bob Murphy birdies the ninth hole, and Grier Jones' wife, Jane, trying to cheer up Murphy's wife, says, "That brings him down, Gail. What's he got for the first nine?"

"When he gets that high," says Gail Murphy, "I quit counting."

Murphy is out in 40, four over par.

11:55 A.M.

On the fifth hole, Gene Littler sinks a twenty-foot putt for a birdie.

12:05 P.M.

After a big drive down the middle of the fairway, Frank Beard birdies the first hole.

12:08 P.M.

In the clubhouse, Arnold Palmer is lacing up a new pair of golf shoes. "How can you risk breaking in a new pair of shoes at the Masters?" a reporter asks.

Palmer looks up. "I start every tournament with a new pair of shoes," he says.

12:10 P.M.

Almost always in the past, when he has played the long second hole, Frank Beard has used a three-wood off the tee, sacrificing distance for safety. But now he takes his driver and gives it a full swing. He hooks his shot into the woods and is forced to settle for a par on a hole he often birdies.

12:18 P.M.

On the short twelfth hole, Jimmy Wright hits his tee shot into the bunker behind the narrow green. He is already two over par and faces a dangerous shot. From his position, the green slopes downhill toward the water. It is almost impossible for him to hold a sand shot anywhere near the pin.

April 9, 1970

Wright blasts the ball out, and it hits the green and rolls off, into the trap separating the putting surface and the brook in front. Again, he blasts out, and this time he stops the ball three feet from the cup. He rolls in the putt and is happy to escape with a bogey-four. "It could've been a six easily," says Wright.

12:23 P.M.

Steve Melnyk and Jack Nicklaus stand on the first tee. "They paired the two heavyweights," the amateur champion says to his playing partner.

"Watch it," says Nicklaus. "I'm not in your class."

For one of the few times in his golfing career, Nicklaus, standing next to Melnyk, looks slender.

"You gonna go on a diet, too?" Nicklaus asks.

"I'm on a diet," says Melnyk, "whenever I don't gain any weight."

12:24 P.M.

Gary Player and his playing partner, Michael Bonallack, the British Amateur champion, reach the fourth tee and find another twosome still waiting to hit. Player sips a cup of water, then walks to the bench on the side of the tee. Four caddies—Player's, Bonallack's and the preceding twosome's—are sitting on the bench. "Room for one more?" Player asks.

The caddies squeeze over—two to the left, two to the right—to make room for Player. He sits down, then glances at the two black caddies on either side of him. "Reporters will pick this up," says the South African, "and it will be in every newspaper in the country."

The spectators laugh, and so do the four caddies.

12:33 P.M.

With a thirty-foot putt, Steve Melnyk birdies the first hole.

12:40 P.M.

On the eighth hole, Gene Littler sinks a four-foot putt for a birdie.

12:48 P.M.

Gracefully, powerfully, artfully, Sam Snead fires his second shot to the thirteenth green. He clears the water easily, hits the green and ends up twenty feet from the pin.

Snead lines up the twenty-footer for an eagle, strokes the ball and misses by four feet. He lines up the four-footer and misses that too. Snead taps in for a par and drops his putter in disgust.

His swing is still magnificent; his putting is still a problem.

1:01 P.M.

With a three-foot putt, Steve Melnyk birdies the third hole to go two under par. "If I don't make any bogeys the rest of the way," he tells himself, "I'll be right up among the leaders."

1:05 P.M.

As he comes off the thirteenth green, after missing a makable putt for the third straight hole, Chi Chi Rodriguez, still one-under for his round, looks at the crowd and explains, "I'm playing like Tarzan—and scoring like Jane."

1:15 P.M.

The wind is swirling around the course, and by now, all the golfers, even the ones who haven't teed off, know that the greens are lightning fast. Arnold Palmer, warming up on the practice green, is cheerful. "This is like the old days around here," he says. "It's going to intimidate a lot of fellows, and you'll have to like the course and know it to hold together."

Palmer smiles. He knows the course and loves it.

1:20 P.M.

Sukree Onsham comes off the eighteenth green and waves to the crowd. He has played the back nine in 36, even-par, and although his opening round of 78 will leave him far behind the leaders, he has shown that a little man can handle at least part of the Augusta course.

April 9, 1970

With three birdies on the last seven holes, Dave Stockton posts a respectable score of 72. "I really enjoyed that pairing," he says. "Sukree's one of the few people in the tournament I can outdrive. It did wonders for my ego to be laying it out there fifty yards beyond him."

Stockton shakes his head. "If only I'd been putting well," he says.

1:25 P.M.

As Tommy Aaron walks from the ninth green to the tenth tee, after shooting a 35 on the front nine, he passes Roberto de Vicenzo coming off the practice green. They nod toward each other. "No, we don't talk about scorecard mistake any more," says de Vicenzo. "People don't mention to me any more about it. Only here."

1:28 P.M.

Larry Hinson, the Georgian in search of an image, finishes his first Masters round with an even-par 72, matching Dave Stockton, who was playing right in front of him. "The way I played," says Hinson, who missed several makable putts, "the worst I could've shot was a 72. Maybe that's a good way to start. I'll be coming back tomorrow feeling the course owes me a few strokes."

1:29 P.M.

On the fifth hole, Steve Melnyk hits his second shot over the green, chips back weakly and three-putts for a double-bogey six. He falls back to even-par for his round.

1:35 P.M.

As Gary Player comes off the eighth green, his escorts clear a path through the gallery. Four of his escorts, wearing Pinkerton uniforms, are unarmed; five others, in civilian clothes, are identifiable by the revolvers bulging in their pants pockets. One of the Pinkertons is drenched in sweat. "What's this?" he says. "The ninth hole? All I'm looking for is the eighteenth."

1:37 P.M.

On the thirteenth hole, Gene Littler sinks a thirty-five-foot putt for a birdie.

1:40 P.M.

As Jimmy Wright leaves the scorer's tent near the eighteenth green after signing for a 75—"I'm a little disappointed," he says, "but it's not too bad for an opener"—several teenagers run up to him for his autograph. "They don't know who I am," he says, "but once they see me sign for one kid, they all come running over."

1:47 P.M.

On the 190-yard sixteenth, Chi Chi Rodriguez puts his tee shot on the green. "What did you hit?" someone yells.

"An eight-iron," says Rodriguez, straight-faced.

"An eight-iron!"

"Yeah," says Chi Chi. "I had cement for breakfast."

1:50 P.M.

Grier Jones finishes his round with a 73, a decent score for a young pro making his Masters debut. "I wasn't hitting the ball well," he says.

His partner, Bob Murphy, comes in with a 78 and a frown, both unusual for him. "I know we'll be on the putting green tonight," says his wife, Gail.

1:57 P.M.

After he belts a long drive off the seventeenth tee, Chi Chi Rodriguez turns to his audience and shouts, "Puerto Rican power. Rice and beans."

The fans laugh. Most of them haven't followed Chi Chi before.

2:05 P.M.

Jack Nicklaus, at even par after a birdie on four and a bogey on six, belts his drive up the right side of the eighth fairway, then

April 9, 1970

takes a three-wood to go for the green with his second shot. He swings, and just before making contact with the ball, his club hits a rock. The club cracks—and the ball stops short of the green. "The rock went farther than the ball," says Nicklaus.

After a brief conference, two Masters officials pick up Nicklaus' three-wood and take it back to the pro shop for emergency repairs.

2:12 P.M.

Chi Chi Rodriguez strokes in his putt for a four on the eighteenth green and becomes the first man in the 1970 Masters to break par. He is in with a 70, which, considering the speed of the greens, and the capriciousness of the wind, is nothing to laugh at.

2:30 P.M.

On the fourteenth hole, Tommy Aaron sinks a fifteen-foot putt for his third consecutive birdie and moves four-under for the round.

2:45 P.M.

More than a third of the golfers have completed their first round in the 1970 Masters, and the early leader, still, is Chi Chi Rodriguez. He sits in front of his locker, with no gallery to play to, and admits that, despite his antics and his wisecracks, he was nervous on the course. "If this was any other tournament but the Masters," says Chi Chi, "I'd have shot a 66. But I was choking out there."

The smiling Puerto Rican, who has gained fifteen or twenty pounds since he stopped smoking cigarettes two years ago—but still doesn't weigh 140—shakes his head. "That green coat," he says, "plays castanets with your knees."

2:47 P.M.

As he walks down the eleventh fairway, Jack Nicklaus receives a present: A Masters official drives up to him in a golf cart and gives him back his repaired three-wood. "I'm glad to get it back," he says. "I've been using this same three-wood since I was an amateur."

2:48 P.M.

On the eighteenth hole, Gene Littler curls in a downhill fifteen-foot putt for a par and a round of 69, four birdies and only one bogey. After all his moaning about his game, he is the first finisher to break 70 in the 1970 Masters.

2:50 P.M.

After playing the first seventeen holes in one stroke under par, Tony Jacklin runs into trouble on the eighteenth. His tee shot lands under a bush, nestled on a bed of pine cones. His second strikes a tree and bounces into the tenth fairway. His third comes to rest on the back of the green, and from there, Jacklin three-putts for a double-bogey and a round of 73. "A 73 with three sixes," says Jacklin, not too happily. "That's an odd round."

3:05 P.M.

The press corps engulfs Gene Littler. Most of the reporters know that he has been worrying about his game all week. They also know that he holds the early first-round lead. What happened?

"Nothing magic," Littler says. "I still haven't found the secret. I scored well, but I can't say I hit the ball well. I took only twenty-seven putts. That can make a good round out of almost anything."

"How was the course?" someone asks.

"There is a definite advantage here," Littler says, "for the man who hits the ball a long way in the air. I don't. I can't say my game is suited to this course."

Littler has nothing more to say, and the reporters drift away. He goes to the practice tee to work on his game—before going home to talk golf with Phil Rodgers, grill a couple steaks and watch TV until bedtime.

April 9, 1970

3:10 P.M.

Playing right behind Tommy Aaron, who is now five-under, Dan Sikes comes to the seventeenth tee four under par, in perfect position to challenge for the lead.

3:14 P.M.

After a round of 75, Takaaki Kono sits in the clubhouse, he and his wife each eating a bacon, lettuce and tomato sandwich, with mashed potatoes on the side, for lunch. "To attend the Masters is a real honor," Kono says, turning to a dish of chocolate ice cream. "I know I'll do better tomorrow."

3:16 P.M.

Billy Casper and his caddy, Matthew Palmer, study the line of a fourteen-foot putt in the eighteenth green. For four straight years, Casper has broken par in the first round of the Masters, and now he needs this fourteen-footer for a one-under-par 71.

The golfer and the caddy whisper suggestions to each other. Then Casper steps up and strokes the ball and it breaks off to the right, below the hole.

"I'm sorry," Matthew Palmer says.

"It's not your fault, Matthew," says Casper. "I just hit it a little weak."

Casper is in with a 72, and for the first time since 1967, he is not the first-round leader in the Masters.

3:20 P.M.

Dan Sikes three-putts on the seventeenth for a bogey.

3:23 P.M.

Tommy Aaron bogeys the eighteenth hole, but finishes with a 68, taking the first-round lead away from Gene Littler.

3:30 P.M.

Dan Sikes three-putts on the eighteenth for his second straight bogey and posts a 70, two strokes off the lead. "Where you going?" someone calls, as Sikes leaves the scorer's tent.

"I'm going to cry," Sikes says.

3:32 P.M.

Billy Casper sits in front of his locker and offers no complaints. "That was a tough golf course out there today," he says. "It was very fast, and very dry, and the greens were difficult to hold. I'm really happy with my round. I feel fortunate to get in with a 72."

"Can you still win?" Casper is asked.

"I think everyone will shoot 72 at least once this week," he says.

3:35 P.M.

With a bogey-five on the seventeenth hole, Gary Player completes a strange stretch of golf. Over the past seven holes, he has shot five fives and two twos—two birdies, two pars and three bogeys.

3:36 P.M.

In the interviewing room, adjacent to the main press room, Tommy Aaron braces himself for the inevitable questions. The question about the scorecard comes first, and Aaron fields it easily. "Sure, I checked my card," he says. "Even when there's only a hundred dollars at stake, I check it."

Then comes the question about Aaron's habit of playing bridesmaid. "I only wish I finished second all the time," he says. "If I did, I'd sure be up there on the money list. Nine second places in ten years of touring isn't all that many, is it?"

Another reporter recalls the de Vicenzo incident, and Aaron, a tall, slender man, calm on the surface, smiles wryly. "I knew I'd be made the heavy," he says. "I felt awful, of course, but it's a rule. A man is responsible for his own score. I wrote down a wrong score and Roberto signed his card without catching it."

"Were you surprised by your score today?" someone asks.

"Yes," says Aaron. "I was surprised at shooting a 68. I don't

April 9, 1970

think anybody expects to shoot a 68 in the opening round of the Masters—not with the greens as fast as they were today."

3:38 P.M.

The word spreads quickly around the course: Arnold Palmer has played the front nine in 35, one under par, and now he is starting the back nine, the scene of his famous charges. His army is swelling—in size and confidence. If anyone can catch Tommy Aaron today, the army figures, it is Arnie.

3:40 P.M.

As Gary Player marches briskly up the center of the eighteenth fairway, two of his plainclothesmen trudge wearily up the side. "These golf shoes are killing me," one says to the other.

3:42 P.M.

Dan Sikes has held back the tears, and now, as he sits in the clubhouse, he is explaining how he three-putted the last two holes. "Both times," he says, "I took too much club and overshot the pin and left myself downhill putts. As hard and fast as these greens are, you have to keep your approach shots below the hole. That's all there is to it. Jack Burke said you could throw a handful of molasses on those greens and it wouldn't hold, and that's about right."

Across the room, Dave Stockton is talking about his own problems on the greens. Sikes eavesdrops and shakes his head. "Everyone out here complains about his own putting," Sikes says, "but Stockton doesn't know how dangerously he's living when he moans. He's such a great putter, someday someone's gonna hit him in the head with a club."

Sikes looks up and sees Gene Sarazen smiling and nodding at him. "He may be smiling at me today," says Sikes, "but oh, tomorrow." Sikes has given an interview to the Associated Press, which carried Sarazen's attack on the touring caddies, and he has defended the caddies. "Gene implies that a golfer would allow his caddy to cheat," Sikes says. "If I caught my caddy cheating,

I'd fire him immediately. I kind of raised one caddy, and after eight years of working for me, he made enough money to go back to college. Without caddying, he couldn't have done that."

3:45 P.M.

Gary Player pars the eighteenth hole and comes in with a 74. "I feel my position is comfortable," he says. "Being six strokes behind with nine holes to go means nothing on this course. I've got fifty-four holes to go."

4:03 P.M.

On the eighteenth tee, big Bob Lunn runs a hand through his thinning reddish hair. He is three under par, and if he can par the final hole, he will tie Gene Littler for second place, only a stroke behind Tommy Aaron. But his second shot on eighteen bounces into the gallery circling the green and, after his recovery, he two-putts for a bogey. Lunn comes in with a 70.

4:05 P.M.

Frank Beard walks toward the clubhouse after shooting a 71. "How long does it take to get from the eighteenth green to the clubhouse?" someone asks him.

"It doesn't take me nearly as long as I'd like it to," says Beard, who is not a prime target for the autograph hunters.

4:15 P.M.

Arnold Palmer bogeys the twelfth hole to slip back to even-par.

4:20 P.M.

As soon as he gets to the clubhouse, Bob Lunn telephones his wife, Angie, in California to let her know about his opening 70 and to ask how she is feeling in the ninth month of her pregnancy.

"Hi, honey," he says, when his wife answers the phone.
"Honey!" she says. "Are you hurt?"

April 9, 1970

"Hurt?"

"I just came from the doctor's," says Angie Lunn, "and on the car radio, I heard the sports news. They said you hit a spectator on the eighteenth green."

Bob Lunn starts to laugh. "No," he says, "I didn't hit a spectator. I wasn't in a fight. I just overshot the eighteenth. My *ball* must've hit someone—not me. No one was hurt."

Angie Lunn tells her husband that her pregnancy is coming along fine, and wishes him luck tomorrow.

4:28 P.M.

Jack Nicklaus bogeys the eighteenth hole and comes in with a scrambling 71. He missed nine of eighteen greens, but made six putts from more than seven feet to preserve his sub-par round.

His amateur playing partner, Steve Melnyk, posts a 73, a creditable score considering that twice Melnyk slipped to double-bogeys. Had he parred those two holes, Melnyk would have had a 69. "I'm very disappointed," Melnyk says. "I could have done much, much better."

4:36 P.M.

Dave Hill, after a 73, is on the putting green, grooving his stroke. A stout, red-faced man named Ray Davis, standing behind the gallery ropes, calls to him, and Hill walks over. "I represent a new cigarette called Venture," Davis says, "and I'd like you to try some."

Davis hands Hill a box holding four cartons of cigarettes. "There's a little book in there tells you all about it," Davis says. "It's a completely different kind of cigarette. In the other cigarettes, the tobacco is poisoned by pesticides, and it's the pesticides that cause coughing and lung cancer. We don't spray our cigarettes with pesticides."

"Thanks," says Hill.

"I wanted you to have some because you smoke the most of all the men on the tour," Davis continues. "You try 'em, and I'm sure you're going to like 'em. Ain't poison like the others."

"Thanks," says Hill. "I'll sure give 'em a try." He hands the cigarettes to his caddy and goes back to practicing his putting.

4:40 P.M.

"Yes, I was nervous," Steve Melnyk says in the clubhouse, "but Jack helped me quite a bit. He helped steady me." Melnyk grins. "So did the birdies," he says.

"Did you ever feel pressure like this before?" someone asks.

"It was worse in the Walker Cup matches," Melnyk says. "They raised the flag and played the national anthem, and I realized I was playing for my country, and I couldn't breathe."

4:50 P.M.

R. H. Sikes is smiling. For the first time in seven appearances at Augusta, he has broken par—with a 70 that puts him only two strokes off the lead. "I hope it's not the last time," says the Arkansas Sikes. "Maybe I'll be able to get me some local knowledge this weekend."

4:58 P.M.

Arnold Palmer three-putts the fifteenth hole for a bogey.

5:01 P.M.

The eighteenth hole, a killer all day, catches another victim: Bruce Devlin. The Australian bogeys the finishing hole, his second straight bogey, and comes in at even-par 72.

5:10 P.M.

Two-under par after fourteen holes, Bert Yancey booms his drive close to 300 yards off the fifteenth tee, down the left side of the fairway, away from the menacing mounds. He studies his second shot to the green. He needs to hit the ball 220 or 230 yards to clear the pond. "What the heck," he says to himself. "Let's go for it."

So far, only four men all day have tried to reach the fifteenth green in two—Nicklaus and Palmer both played short—

April 9, 1970

and only one has succeeded: Dr. Cary Middlecoff, forty-nine years old, the winner of the 1955 Masters. The other three carried the water, but failed to hold the green. Yancey follows their example.

He takes his three-wood and hits the ball solidly. It clears the pond by a comfortable margin, but bounces into a bunker on the right of the green. Then he blasts out and sinks a four-foot putt to go three-under for the day.

5:12 P.M.

After an hour and a half of practice, Bob Murphy walks off the putting green. He knows that he will have to shoot par or better tomorrow, or he will not be around for the final two rounds of the Masters.

5:17 P.M.

For the eighth time in his last nine competitive rounds at Augusta, Bert Yancey birdies the short sixteenth hole. He is now four under par for his round, and if he can par the last two holes, he will tie Tommy Aaron for the lead.

5:38 P.M.

Arnold Palmer three-putts the eighteenth hole for his second straight bogey, his fourth in six holes, and staggers in with a 75. "I'm not crazy about the score," he says. "I'll give it to anyone who wants it."

Palmer no longer is in love with the course. "Those fairways," he grumbles, shaking his head.

His playing partner, Vinnie Giles, would be willing to take a 75. Giles, the only amateur to break 290 in the Masters in the past seven years, finishes three strokes behind Palmer at 78.

5:44 P.M.

On the seventeenth hole, Bert Yancey fires his second shot to within eighteen inches of the cup. He practically has a tap-in for a birdie that will put him five-under, that will give him the first-round lead all by himself. He looks at the putt and starts thinking about the crystal vase that is presented to the player who turns in the lowest score for each round of the Masters.

Then he steps up to the ball, strokes it and misses. "I guess I was thinking more about the vase than the putt," Yancey admits. "I know my wife wanted it very badly."

5:54 P.M.

Bob Lunn is standing on the putting green as Arnold Palmer marches past on his way to the clubhouse. "You know," Lunn says, "that man made golf what it is today. Ken Still once told me that if he were in the locker room, and Arnie wanted his shoes shined, he'd take off his shirt and shine them. So would I."

5:48 P.M.

Only one year too late, Charlie Coody strokes in a putt on the final green to give him pars for the sixteenth, seventeenth and eighteenth holes. He finishes with a 70. "I had no thoughts about last year," Coody says, "when I played sixteen, seventeen and eighteen. Of course, the situation was entirely different. The pressure on Thursday's not quite the same as on Sunday."

Coody is proof of the theory that the most important asset at Augusta is experience. He is playing in his fifth Masters, and his opening round scores have been, in order, 80, 78, 76, 74 and now 70.

"I feel looser than I've felt in three or four weeks," Coody says. "I've got two doctors from back home in Abilene staying with me here, and they've got me taking hot baths and hot showers and muscle relaxants, and I'm really feeling good." The 70 didn't hurt any, either.

5:58 P.M.

Bert Yancey, wearing dark-green slacks and a green-striped shirt, is still four-under as he steps to the eighteenth tee. On the eighteenth, based on his careful study of the course, he usually hits a three-wood off the tee. Now he asks his caddy for his driver.

April 9, 1970

He has heard that Arnold Palmer finished half an hour earlier with a 75. "If I'd made that putt on seventeen," Yancey tells himself, "I'd be eight strokes ahead of Arnie."

While he ponders the likelihood of beating Palmer so badly, Yancey pulls his drive to the left of a fairway bunker.

5:59 P.M.

Roberto de Vicenzo comes off the eighteenth green, still smiling, but shaking his head. "No too good this time," he says. The Argentine checks his scorecard and signs, accurately, for a 78.

6:01 P.M.

On the eighteenth, Bert Yancey's second shot hits a spectator and bounces into a trap guarding the green. He blasts out and two-putts for a bogey.

He is still six strokes ahead of Arnie, but, at 69, he is one stroke behind Tommy Aaron and tied with Gene Littler for second place.

"From tee to green," Yancey says, "I played as well as I've ever played in my life."

His wife, Linda, will have to get along without a crystal vase.

6:10 P.M.

Homero Blancas, who played with Bert Yancey and shot an 81—the highest score recorded all day by anyone who plays the pro tour regularly, and the same score shot by Gene Sarazen—thinks he knows why he had so much trouble. "The way I putted," Blancas says, "I must've been reading the greens in Spanish and putting them in English."

6:15 P.M.

A battery of reporters surrounds Bert Yancey, peppering him with questions about his round. "Why do you wear green so much?" a newspaperman asks.

"I like green," Yancey says. "I'm not afraid to wear green here. I'm not afraid to win this tournament."

8:45 P.M.

Steve Melnyk is in bed, reading *The Godfather*. "I think I've got hay fever," he says to his roommate, Vinnie Giles. "Those pine trees are bothering me." He is suffering worse from double-bogeys.

9:45 P.M.

In a private club atop a bank building in downtown Augusta, Dan Sikes and his wife are attending a small dinner party. One of the guests at their table is Tennessee Ernie Ford, and when everyone finishes eating, Tennessee Ernie leads them in group singing. "Now that's what I call class," says the Florida Sikes, "bringing your own entertainment."

Sikes laughs, thoroughly enjoying himself. It isn't difficult to be cheerful after a sub-par round on the opening day of the Masters.

THE LEADERS AFTER THE FIRST ROUND

Tommy Aaron	68
Gene Littler	69
Bert Yancey	69
Chi Chi Rodriguez	70
Dan Sikes	70
Bob Lunn	70
R. H. Sikes	70
Charles Coody	70
Frank Beard	71
Jack Nicklaus	71
Larry Hinson	72
Dave Stockton	72
Billy Casper	72
Bruce Devlin	72
Grier Jones	73
Dave Hill	73
Tony Jacklin	73
George Knudson	73
Al Geiberger	73
Steve Melnyk	73
Tom Weiskopf	73
George Archer	73
Orville Moody	73

FRIDAY

April 10, 1970

Three 68s from Three Continents

T̲he pressure is building—twin pressures, pressure to stay among the leaders and pressure to stay among the competitors. Anyone who wants to remain in serious contention for the championship figures he must, after two rounds, be no worse than 144, no worse than even-par. In the history of the Masters, only five men have finished first after being over par at the halfway mark; no one has done it in the past ten years.

For Gary Player, at 74, this means he must shoot 70 or better. Arnold Palmer, at 75, must break 70. Palmer and Player have good company among those who must show drastic improvement to challenge for the title. Ten men who finished among the top twenty-four last year shot rounds of 74 or worse yesterday: Harold Henning and Deane Beman, at 74; Lionel Hebert, Bruce Crampton and Takaaki Kono, at 75; Don January, Miller Barber, Mason Rudolph and Dale Douglass, at 76; and Jack Burke, Jr., at 78.

Anyone who wants to remain in the competition for the final thirty-six holes figures he must, after two rounds, be no worse than 150. In the Masters, only the leading forty-four golfers, plus ties, survive the halfway cut, and forty-three men shot 75 or better yesterday. (*There is one exception to the rule of forty-four: Anyone within ten strokes of the leader after thirty-six holes plays the last two rounds. But it is unusual for more than forty-four players to remain within ten strokes of first place.*)

The roster of players who will have to rally dramatically to survive the cut includes nearly a dozen former champions, every former champion in the field except Nicklaus, Palmer, Player and Archer. The 1968 champion, Bob Goalby, is at 77, and the 1967 champion, Gay Brewer, and the 1968 runner-up, Roberto de Vicenzo, are both at 78.

The only 1970 starter who is under no pressure at all is Henry Picard, the 1938 Masters champion. He doesn't have to worry about bogeys or birdies today: After shooting a 41 on the front nine yesterday, Picard, who is sixty-two years old, withdrew from the tournament.

7:10 A.M.

Bob Lunn steps out of his room at the Holiday Inn and starts downstairs to pick up a morning paper. Five years ago, he recalls, he was home in California, living above a garage, sleeping in a foldout bed that sometimes would open up only after an hour of tugging. In those days, Lunn had a ten-year-old Cadillac that he parked facing downhill every night so that he'd have enough momentum to get it going in the morning. He was a teaching pro at a driving range then, and now he earns more than $75,000 a year on the tour.

Lunn is wearing Levis, a T-shirt and alligator loafers. The Levis are baggy; in the three and a half weeks since his wife left the tour, to go home to await their second child, Lunn has lost fifteen pounds, from 225 down to 210.

"Hey, Bob," a friend calls, as Lunn enters the motel lobby, "that's a great outfit to wear to the Masters."

April 10, 1970

8:05 A.M.

Steve Melnyk sits in the dining room in the upstairs locker room, almost completely surrounded by his breakfast—steak, eggs, potatoes, juice and coffee. "Breakfast costs only a buck for the amateurs," he says. "Might as well eat up." A few other golfers seated nearby stare at Melnyk, as awed as if he had just pounded a 300-yard drive.

9:15 A.M.

The svelte Jack Nicklaus treats himself to his version of a big breakfast: Bacon, eggs, melon, toast and milk. "I won't eat again until this evening," he apologizes.

9:20 A.M.

Whenever Charlie Coody feels he needs to shoot a strong round, he puts on his good-luck charm: A pair of red socks. Most weeks, he waits until Sunday, payday, to bolster his luck, but this week is different. This is the Masters. As he walks to the practice tee before his second round, Coody is wearing red socks. "Gonna make a run at the leaders today," he says.

9:30 A.M.

Shirley Casper sets breakfast down in front of her husband: Three sliced oranges and half a pompano. It is not quite so dramatic as the buffalo meat Billy Casper has been known to eat.

Usually, Casper skips breakfast before a round, but because he is not teeing off until 12:30 today, he feels the early meal won't hurt him. "If you're hungry," he explains, "you're more alert. You're like a hungry lion. All your senses are sharpened for the kill."

10:40 A.M.

On the veranda, facing the practice tee, Gail Murphy is watching her husband, Bob, putting. "Well," says Gail, "we're going to try a new putter today. We have about twelve of them, but none of them feels right."

10:50 A.M.

After pars on the first hole, Bert Yancey and Charlie Coody, paired together, both birdie the second. Another triumph for the copper bracelet and the red socks.

11 A.M.

The big scoreboard adjacent to the eighteenth fairway shows the current leaders:

PLAYER	HOLES	SCORE
Aaron	18	—4
Yancey	20	—4
Littler	18	—3
Coody	20	—3

11:03 A.M.

Bruce Devlin stands in front of his locker, trying on a new golf glove, an Arnold Palmer glove bearing the Palmer symbol —a multicolored umbrella—on the back. Devlin tests the glove, likes the way it feels and decides he'll use it. But before he goes to the practice tee, he rips the umbrella symbol off the glove. He is not going to give Arnie free advertising. "Tell him to pay me and I'll leave it on," says Devlin, with a grin. "Even a dollar a day. That'll be enough."

11:45 A.M.

A reporter cruising the practice tee asks Billy Casper if he can tell from his practice swings whether or not he's "on."

"I can't tell until I've played seventeen holes," Casper says. "Then I get some kind of idea."

11:54 A.M.

Bert Yancey and Charlie Coody both bogey the seventh hole. For Yancey, it is his first bogey of the day; for Coody, it is his third in a row, dropping him far from the leaders and proving that copper is stronger than cotton.

April 10, 1970

12 NOON
The current leaders:

PLAYER	HOLES	SCORE
Aaron	18	−4
Yancey	25	−3
Littler	18	−3

12:20 P.M.
On the practice tee, Chi Chi Rodriguez turns to the gallery, then points at Larry Ziegler. "I once saw that guy hit a drive 570 yards," Chi Chi chirps. He whistles in awe. "On a par-three hole," he adds.

12:48 P.M.
Bert Yancey doesn't even think about playing the eleventh hole safe, to the right side of the green, away from the stream. He shoots right for the flag, reaches the green and knocks in a fifteen-foot putt for a birdie. He is back to one-under for the day.

12:55 P.M.
Chi Chi Rodriguez hits a big drive off the second tee, turns to the crowd, waves his arms over his head and announces, "Chi Chi Palmer."

The Puerto Rican shakes his head. "I don't see how the ball can take it," he says.

12:58 P.M.
On the twelfth hole, the demanding par-three tucked behind Rae's Creek, Bert Yancey goes boldly for the pin and comes within ten feet of his target. He rams in his putt for a birdie-two.

1 P.M.
The current leaders:

PLAYER	HOLES	SCORE
Yancey	30	−5
Aaron	18	−4
Lunn	28	−3
Littler	18	−3

1:02 P.M.

Dave Stockton, concentrating on fighting off attacks of nervousness, faces an eight-foot birdie putt on the second hole. He measures it carefully, taps it and sinks it. Suddenly, he feels a great deal calmer.

1:13 P.M.

On the par-five thirteenth hole, Bert Yancey reaches the green in two and two-putts for his third consecutive birdie, moving six-under for the tournament.

1:21 P.M.

Vinnie Giles faces an eighteen-foot putt on the final green. He needs to sink the putt for a round of even-par 72 and a thirty-six hole total of 150.

"You make that putt," says his playing partner, Mason Rudolph, "you'll make the cut."

"No way," says Giles. "The cut's not going to be that high."

Then Giles strokes the putt into the cup. "I hope you're right," he says to Rudolph.

1:22 P.M.

As he walks down the fifteenth fairway to his long drive, Steve Melnyk is two over par for his round, three-over for the Masters. He has readjusted his sights from the victory he sought before the tournament began. "All I've got to do," he thinks, "is stay out of the water here, and I've got the cut made."

He reaches the drive and studies the distance to the green. "I can't lay up," he figures. "I'll look like a fool—or a coward."

Melnyk takes his four-wood and goes for the green. But he catches the ball in the neck of the club. His shot splashes into the pond, and he takes a bogey-six.

1:23 P.M.

It is probably the strangest pairing of the day: The smiling flyweight from Japan, Takaaki Kono, and the dour millionaire

April 10, 1970

from West Virginia, Sam Snead, move to the first tee, both worrying about making the cut. Kono shot 75 yesterday, Snead a stroke higher. Someone suggests they ought to get along well, because they both speak only broken English.

1:24 P.M.

Frank Beard and Chi Chi Rodriguez come to the fourth tee. They have each parred the first three holes, and as they await their turn to tee off, Chi Chi keeps up a running conversation with nearby spectators. "The last time I played here," Chi Chi says, "I was listed as one of the foreign players. Then they found out Puerto Rico was part of the United States."

The fans howl; Beard stares at the ground.

"You know," Chi Chi says, "I once hit a drive 500 yards."

"Really?" someone says.

"Sure," says Rodriguez. "On a par-three hole."

The crowd roars, and Chi Chi adds, "I had a three-wood coming back."

Then he double-bogeys the fourth hole to fall back to even-par for the tournament. But, as he walks off the green, Chi Chi is still smiling, still chattering. Beard is still straight-faced.

1:25 P.M.

Gene Littler is paired with Gary Player, but the presence of Gary's Guards, the uniformed Pinkertons and the plainclothesmen, does not seem to be upsetting the quiet Californian. On the second hole, he rolls in an eight-foot putt for his second straight birdie. He goes five-under for the tournament.

1:28 P.M.

With a frown on his face, Bob Rosburg walks out to the scoreboard next to the first fairway. He has shot a 73, after an opening 77, and he wants to calculate his chances of making the cut. He looks over the scores of the handful of players who have finished, and he is not encouraged by what he sees. Terry Wilcox, who opened with a 79, has followed with a 70; England's Maurice Bembridge, who opened with a 77, has followed with a 72. The front-nine scores for the later starters are running lower than yesterday. Rosburg figures it will take a score of 149 or better to survive the cut. He goes back to his rented house to pack his bags and get ready to leave Augusta. "It'll take a miracle for me to make the cut," Rosburg says.

1:35 P.M.

After a strong drive on the par-five eighth hole, Jack Nicklaus studies his next shot. He decides he can go for the green, and he pulls out his three-wood, the same club that he cracked on this hole yesterday.

Nicklaus addresses the ball, swings and hooks his shot. The ball sails deep into the woods on the left of the fairway. Nicklaus trudges up the fairway, then turns into the woods. The forecaddie, a few Masters officials and several dozen spectators are already searching for his ball.

1:36 P.M.

Once again, Bert Yancey, who does not think of himself as a power hitter, is in position to try for the fifteenth green with his second shot. If he can slice a stroke off par here, he will go seven-under for the tournament. He might even win a crystal vase for Linda.

He hits a three-wood and clears the pond—by thirty or forty inches. Still short of the green, Yancey chips up, takes two putts and stays at six-under.

"It probably wasn't worth the risk," Yancey says of his bid for the green. "There was a little breeze against me."

1:37 P.M.

On the thirteenth hole, Bob Lunn picks up a birdie, his second of the back nine, and, at four-under for the tournament, remains solidly in contention for the Masters championship.

April 10, 1970

1:38 P.M.

Steve Melnyk bogeys the sixteenth hole and goes four-over for his round.

1:44 P.M.

Jack Nicklaus gives up. He cannot find his ball. "I don't think anyone in the gallery picked it up," he says. He spots some holes in the ground, probably left by old tree roots, and he reasons that his ball disappeared down one of the holes. The ball might have gone into a swamp in the woods, but Nicklaus and his gallery have practically dredged the swamp searching for the ball.

Nicklaus drops a new ball, then hooks his next shot into a bunker. He is lying four, and he still hasn't reached the green. He blasts out of the bunker to within fifteen feet of the pin—and then three-putts for a horrendous triple-bogey eight, dropping him far out of contention for the lead.

"I've made some sixes on the par-threes here," Nicklaus says, unhappily, "but I can't remember ever making an eight."

1:49 P.M.

Bert Yancey steps to the tee at the sixteenth hole, the hole he owns, the hole he has birdied eight times in his last nine tries. "Let's get another birdie now," he tells himself.

He studies the pin, tucked in the right rear of the green. There is plenty of room to play safe in front of the pin, but Yancey's adrenalin is flowing. He is thinking only of charging, only of gaining on par.

He takes a four-iron and swings. The ball, off-line, sails to the right of the green and comes to rest among brown pine needles, near a trap guarding the right rear of the green.

"I tried to hit it too easy," Yancey tells his caddy. "I should've used a five-iron."

He chips onto the green, but skids twenty-five feet past the pin. Yancey two-putts and surrenders a stroke to par.

1:55 P.M.

"Tough luck, Homero," a friend calls to Homero Blancas, who is packing his clubs into his car outside the clubhouse. Blancas has come in at 155, far too high to survive the cut.

"Anyway," says Blancas, pleasantly, "I was low Mexican."

1:57 P.M.

On the par-three sixth hole, Dave Stockton rolls in a twenty-foot birdie putt to move two-under for his round and two-under for the tournament.

2 P.M.

The current leaders:

PLAYER	HOLES	SCORE
Yancey	34	−5
Littler	23	−4
Lunn	32	−4
Aaron	20	−3
Stockton	24	−2

2:01 P.M.

Grier Jones comes to the short twelfth hole, two over par for his round, three-over for the tournament. Knowing he must charge now to get in contention, he strokes his iron boldly for the pin. The ball splashes into the water.

Jones takes his penalty stroke and chips onto the green. Then he two-putts for a double-bogey that lifts him to five-over. With six holes to go, he realizes that he is in danger of missing the cut.

Tex Jones, Grier's father, walks over to Jane Jones, Grier's wife, and puts his arm around her shoulder. "C'mon," he says. "Don't worry. It's not too bad."

2:04 P.M.

The 1970 amateur challenge is dead. Steve Melnyk comes in with a 76 for a total of 149 and is not even positive he'll make

April 10, 1970

the cut. His playing partner, Tom Weiskopf, posts his second straight 73 and isn't particularly pleased, either. "Steve," Weiskopf says, as the two big hitters move off the eighteenth green, "I think we forgot to take the covers off our putters."

"Even if I don't make the cut," Melnyk says, "I've enjoyed playing here. They do everything so perfectly here. Every other tournament's got to be a letdown after this one."

2:17 P.M.

Bob Lunn, two under par for his round and four-under for the tournament, hits a good drive off the seventeenth tee and pulls a small box of raisins out of his golf bag. He shakes some raisins into his mouth. "My wife eats them all the time," Lunn says, "so I thought I'd try them. They're good for energy. I've been eating them for two rounds, and I haven't felt tired."

2:18 P.M.

On the long thirteenth, Grier Jones wins a stroke back from par with a birdie putt, and his father and his wife both beam. Now, barring disaster, he seems likely to make the cut.

2:20 P.M.

With pars on the seventeenth and eighteenth holes, Bert Yancey posts a 70 and a thirty-six hole total of 139. He walks off the eighteenth green holding the Masters lead.

2:21 P.M.

Sitting in the lower locker room, staring at a closed-circuit telecast of the action on the course—a CBS warmup for the nationwide show tomorrow and Sunday—Vinnie Giles lets out a groan. "That knocks me out," he says.

He has just watched Bert Yancey sink his putt for a par on the eighteenth. Like the one other player who is in at 150—Bob Rosburg—Giles was frankly pulling for Yancey to bogey the eighteenth. If no one shot better than 140, then everybody at 150 and under would make the cut.

2:22 P.M.

On the short fourth hole, Tommy Aaron takes a five—his fourth straight five. He now has bogey, par, bogey, double-bogey, and in less than an hour, he has lost all four of the strokes he took away from par yesterday.

The four consecutive fives don't do much for Aaron's pride, but they certainly make it easy for him to add up his scorecard.

2:35 P.M.

The big Argentine smiles. "I don't think I play tomorrow," he says. "I shoot 73 today." Roberto de Vicenzo is at 151 for thirty-six holes, and he realizes that unless all the players on the course collapse or add up their scores incorrectly, he has missed the cut for the second straight year since his historic error.

"What would you do," someone asks, "if you had another scorecard crisis here?"

"Next time?" says de Vicenzo. "Next time, I bring my lawyer."

2:38 P.M.

Bert Yancey sits in the interviewing room, flashing his copper bracelet at the reporters gathered in front of him. "I just love to play golf on this course," he says. "If I play a bad hole, like I did on sixteen, I just look forward to playing the next hole. I enjoy the whole thing, the azaleas and the water and the crowds, and when you feel like that, you can't get too scared out there."

Yancey pauses. "Instead of being afraid," he adds, "I'm enjoying myself."

A reporter shifts the subject. "Were you sick last week at Greensboro?" he asks.

At Greensboro, Yancey shot a 78 in the first round and then dropped out of the tournament.

"No," says Yancey, "I was obsessed with the Masters."

The former West Point cadet stops and thinks, and his expression turns serious. "I felt OK," he says. "I wasn't hurt or

April 10, 1970

sick or anything. I just wanted to come on down to Augusta and work on my putting. Somehow, I just felt it was important to get here. I went to the sponsor and told him just that. I didn't lie. I was under the impression I had the sponsor's permission to leave.

"I know there's some penalty for pulling out of a tournament without just cause, but I left anyway. It was one of the worst things I've ever done, and I'll never do it again. Nobody should withdraw from a tournament if he's physically able to play."

2:39 P.M.

On the tenth hole, Billy Casper strokes a nine-iron 134 yards—"That's exact," says Casper, "not an estimate"—to the green, then raps in a six-foot putt for a birdie. He goes two-under for the round and the tournament.

2:40 P.M.

Charlie Coody walks into the lower locker room and pulls off his golf shoes, exposing his red socks. They didn't work their magic today. Charlie is at even-par, 144, after a disappointing 74. Someone asks Coody what went wrong.

"I took thirty-eight putts," he says. "That won't win any ribbons."

2:41 P.M.

His putter blazing now, Dave Stockton sinks a fifteen-footer for a birdie on the ninth hole, his second birdie in a row, his third in four holes, and goes four-under for the 1970 Masters. The California fisherman is only one stroke off the lead.

2:50 P.M.

Outside the press tent, Bert Yancey meets Joseph Dey, the commissioner of the Tournament Players Division of the PGA. The two of them chat briefly, then disappear into the office of Colonel Homer Shields.

2:54 P.M.

Bob Murphy, using his new putter, completes a round of 70, matching the low score of the day so far, and comfortably makes the cut at 148.

2:58 P.M.

On the ninth green, Gary Player raises his fist in triumph and watches his twenty-foot putt fall into the cup for his third straight birdie and his fifth of the front nine. With only one bogey to mar his string, he is four-under for the round, two-under for the tournament, once again in position to challenge for his second Masters championship.

3 P.M.

The current leaders:

PLAYER	HOLES	SCORE
Yancey	36	−5
Littler	27	−5
Lunn	36	−4
Stockton	28	−3
Casper	29	−2
Player	27	−2

3:02 P.M.

On the seventh hole, Takaaki Kono, five-foot-six and roughly 140 pounds, an incredibly gifted iron player, hits his second shot within a foot of the cup. A year ago, Kono became the first golfer ever to eagle the seventeenth hole at Augusta; now, he has come within twelve inches of the first eagle in the history of the seventh hole.

Kono taps in his putt for a birdie, his third birdie in four holes.

3:04 P.M.

When Bert Yancey and Joe Dey emerge from their private meeting, the commissioner announces that he has fined Yancey

April 10, 1970

$150, the minimum penalty, for withdrawing from the Greater Greensboro Open without permission. "It was a misunderstanding," Dey says. "He thought he had the sponsor's permission to withdraw."

Yancey seems relieved that he has been reprimanded so lightly. For a moment, he had a terrible fear that, because of his actions at Greensboro, he might be disqualified from the golf tournament he considers the most important in the world.

3:05 P.M.

First, his drive catches a fairway bunker on the eighteenth. Then, his second shot catches one of the bunkers guarding the green. Finally, Arnold Palmer blasts out and takes two putts for a bogey and comes in with a 73, giving him a halfway total of 148, nine strokes behind the leader.

His army retreats from the course.

3:11 P.M.

Dave Stockton's eight-iron fails to reach the twelfth green, and for the second time in three holes, he has to settle for a bogey.

3:12 P.M.

"I played like a cow," says Tony Jacklin as he emerges from the scorer's tent, after signing for a 74. "I could have had an 80."

His playing partner, Arnold Palmer, offers Jacklin some consolation. "Look," Palmer says, "the first time we played together here, three years ago, I'd never even heard of you. Now you're the British Open champion."

Someone asks Palmer about his putting, and the king shakes his head. "I can see the line," he says, "but I just can't make it go there. That's my problem."

3:19 P.M.

On the eighth hole, Takaaki Kono rams in a five-foot putt for his fourth birdie in five holes.

3:20 P.M.

Ray Floyd, the PGA champion who had no difficulty with the Augusta course during his practice rounds, walks into the lower locker room. "How'd you do, Ray?" someone asks.

"I'm going home," says Floyd.

He has shot his second 76, and he knows he cannot possibly survive the cut. "After that round yesterday," he says, "I still had it in my mind I could win this tournament."

Floyd, who is down to 180 pounds, from 200, after switching from whiskey to white wine, slumps in front of his locker. "Had a helluva lot of chances," he says, "but I just couldn't get the ball in the hole."

Across the room, Bob Lunn, holding second place among the men who have finished thirty-six holes, looks at Floyd sympathetically. "Last year at this time," says Lunn, "I was packing my bags to go home."

In 1969, in his first Masters appearance, Lunn shot 149 and missed the cut by a stroke. "The wind was blowing last year, and I tried to hit the ball low," he says. "Now the wind is blowing, but I'm playing my own game. I'm keeping the ball pretty high. It seems to be working out OK."

3:23 P.M.

On the eighteenth green, Jimmy Wright lines up a ten-foot putt, strokes it and misses. "I wish I'd holed that," Wright says. "I'd like to be able to say I'd broken par at Augusta."

Wright is in with a 72, and a halfway total of 147, a cinch to survive the cut. "That takes care of one of my goals," he says. "Now I have to go out and finish in the top twenty-four." Wright realizes that since the odds are heavy against his placing high in the U.S. Open or the PGA this year, finishing among the top twenty-four is the easiest way for him to earn a return trip to the Masters next year.

"The putting here is unbelievable," he says. "I can't remember ever having seven- and eight-footers for birdies and not really trying hard to make them. I lag the ball up, sort of,

April 10, 1970

and hope it goes in. You have to cozy the ball in there to make sure you don't three-putt."

Wright glances back at the course with respect. "Anywhere but here," he says, "my round was good enough to be a 68."

3:30 P.M.

"How do you feel now?" a reporter asks Bert Yancey in the locker room.

"I think I'm going to put four good rounds together," Yancey says.

He slips off his golf shoes and looks up. "I don't *think*," says Yancey. "I *know*."

3:33 P.M.

He still may not have an image, but as he comes off the eighteenth green, Larry Hinson has his second straight 72. He now stands third among all the players who have finished. Roughly half the field is in, and only Bert Yancey and Bob Lunn have sub-par totals.

3:35 P.M.

Tommy Aaron stands on the tenth tee, dejected and discouraged. This morning, he was leading the Masters, and now he is barely among the top ten. He has managed to par the fifth through ninth holes only by scrambling; twice, he needed one-putt greens to preserve his pars.

"This is the kind of course," Aaron thinks, "on which you can keep making bogeys. You shoot 40 on the front nine and you might shoot 40 on the back nine, too."

3:40 P.M.

As Bert Yancey comes out of the clubhouse, ready to leave the club, Will Grimsley, the golf expert of the Associated Press, walks up to him. "Bert," says Grimsley, "isn't it true that you like to put yourself in an isolation booth, that you like to close yourself off from everything when you play here?"

"Not really," says Yancey.

Grimsley persists. "Aren't you in some sort of a trance when you're playing the Masters?" he asks.

"What did you say?" says Yancey, deadpan.

3:42 P.M.

Marching down the thirteenth fairway, Chi Chi Rodriguez walks over by the gallery ropes, and his wife hands him a Gelusil tablet. "I need this," Chi Chi announces to the crowd. "I've got enough gas to go from here to New York, nonstop."

Rodriguez is five-over for his round, but nothing quiets him down.

3:45 P.M.

With an eight-foot putt, Tommy Aaron birdies the difficult tenth hole and edges back to one stroke under par.

3:51 P.M.

"Ave Maria!" Chi Chi Rodriguez shouts, as he hits a booming drive off the fourteenth tee. "I don't see how the ball can take it." Chi Chi grins. "When I hit it," he says, "smoke comes out."

Smoke is also coming out of Chi Chi's playing partner, Frank Beard, who takes his golf very seriously. Beard has neither laughed nor scored a birdie so far all day. And on the fourteenth, after an errant tee shot, Beard takes a double-bogey six and goes four-over for his round, three-over for the tournament, far behind the leaders.

"That fella," says a spectator, nodding toward Chi Chi, "is worth the price of admission."

Frank Beard doesn't agree.

3:59 P.M.

Tommy Aaron strokes in a forty-foot putt on the eleventh hole for his second straight birdie. "Now, that's a little better," he tells himself.

April 10, 1970

4:07 P.M.

Bruce Devlin pulls off his Arnold Palmer glove and sits down in front of his locker. He has made the cut easily, with a 74 for 146, but for the second day in a row, he has bogeyed both the seventeenth and eighteenth holes. Take away those four strokes, and Devlin would be bidding for the Masters championship.

Ironically, on the eleventh hole, the hole that cost him the Masters championship two years ago, Devlin has scored two pars.

4:16 P.M.

As he steps off the seventeenth green, Billy Casper has a pretty good idea of how he's doing: He has just sunk his third birdie putt of twenty-five feet or longer, and he is now four-under for the round and the tournament. He is only one stroke behind Bert Yancey, the leader in the clubhouse, and Gene Littler, the leader on the course.

4:18 P.M.

"I lost a ball and took thirty-eight putts," says Jack Nicklaus. "It's as simple as that."

He shakes his head. He doesn't like his 75 any more than his followers do, but he understands perfectly how it happened. In addition to his triple-bogey eight on the eighth hole, he twice three-putted for bogeys.

Yesterday, he hit only nine greens in regulation and, his putter hot, shot 71. Today, he hit fifteen greens in regulation and, his putter useless, shot 75.

"Maybe tomorrow," Nicklaus says, "I'll make those putts, shoot 67 and be back in the game."

4:24 P.M.

Swinging easily again, not pressing, Tommy Aaron reaches the thirteenth green in two shots and two-putts for his third birdie in four holes. As swiftly as he fell out of the lead, he is challenging once more.

4:32 P.M.

For the second time today, Japan's Takaaki Kono comes within a foot of an eagle. He settles for a birdie on the thirteenth hole.

4:35 P.M.

As Billy Casper emerges from the scorer's tent, after carefully adding and signing his card, Shirley Casper waves to him. "Nice round," she calls. Her husband has shot a 68, the low score of the day so far.

"Hi," says Casper, nodding blankly at his wife. He hops into a golf cart and rides off to the press tent.

"He's still in a daze," Shirley Casper says. "He still thinks he's on the course. It usually takes him half an hour or forty-five minutes to recognize people, to come back to reality."

4:36 P.M.

With a double-bogey on eighteen, Dave Stockton completes a strange round of 72—32 going out and 40 coming in. "The double-bogey doesn't bother me that much," he says. "On this course, you're going to get one now and then, and mine just happened to come on the last hole. It could've come earlier. I was just playing from hole to hole. I think I made such a big effort to control my nerves early in the round that it took something out of me, and I finished badly. I got mentally tired on the back side."

4:43 P.M.

Frank Beard and Chi Chi Rodriguez each bogey the eighteenth hole and come in with identical scores of 76, dropping them both out of the top fifteen. Chi Chi still looks cheerful; Beard looks grim, but he has one consolation: He knows the odds are high that he won't be paired with Chi Chi again in the 1970 Masters.

April 10, 1970

4:41 P.M.

Hsieh Yung-Yo, a Nationalist Chinese who works as a golf pro in Tokyo, lines up a birdie putt on the eighteenth green. His English is minimal, but his arithmetic is fine. He knows that if he can sink the putt, he will come in with 150 and have a chance of making the cut. If he misses the putt, he can start checking the flight schedules to the Orient.

He strokes the putt gently, and the ball rolls up to the cup and falls in. Hsieh Yung-Yo beams. "I birdie eighteen," he says, "one time out of one hundred."

His playing partner, Dave Hill, comes in with a 70 and, at 143, trails the leader in the clubhouse, Bert Yancey, by only four strokes.

4:55 P.M.

On the eighteenth green, Gene Littler and Gary Player both tap in putts for pars. Littler finishes with a 70, tying Bert Yancey for the halfway lead at 139, and Player finishes with a 68, tying Billy Casper for low round of the day.

4:58 P.M.

Jack Nicklaus is on the practice tee, firing ball after ball down the range, searching for his groove. "There's a guy," says another pro, "who flat isn't going to tolerate any further decline in his game. He knows if he does, he'll be back with the rest of us."

5:08 P.M.

Larry Ziegler comes off the eighteenth green, his usual smile replaced by a scowl. His wife, Joanne, and his infant daughter, Susan, are waiting for him, and neither of them looks happy, either.

But Ziegler still has his sense of humor. "Well," he says, "I was wrong."

After his opening 76 yesterday, he said, "I can't play any

worse than that." And today he has posted a 78. For the third week in a row, he has failed to survive the halfway cut.

"I'm not going to stick around here," he says. "We're leaving in the morning. The Masters is over for me. I don't even care who wins."

Ziegler pauses. "Well," he says, "I would like to see Lit win. I like Gene. We're good friends." And then he gathers his wife and his child and packs all his equipment in his car.

5:10 P.M.

Gary Player is discussing his round with the press. He is happy with his score, he admits, but not quite satisfied. "I was five-under playing the fifteenth," he says, "and I went for the green on my second. I made it across, but I was in the bunker. I chipped a little short—that water is waiting, you know—and three-putted for a bogey.

"It was hard to take, let me tell you. Here everybody is laying up in front of the water, and I knock it over and still make a bogey. A birdie there would've meant 66."

Even the best sand blasters can't always get down in two out of the Augusta bunkers.

5:14 P.M.

"Honest," says Gene Littler, reviewing his round, "I'm still not hitting the ball what I'd call well. I admit it's better, and I guess scoring so well makes me feel pretty good about things. I didn't putt as super as I did yesterday, but you can never go out expecting to get around with only twenty-seven putts. I'm putting well enough, though, to be in better shape for the Masters than I've been in my sixteen other years."

Never before, in sixty-one rounds at Augusta, has Gene Littler held even a share of the Masters lead at the end of any one day's play.

5:15 P.M.

After a 77 that has just about killed his championship chances, Dan Sikes heads straight for the practice tee. He hits a

April 10, 1970

large bag of balls, then waves his caddy in. As the caddy reaches him, Sikes says, "Let me have just one more ball."

Fourteen times, Sikes repeats the same request. Finally, he turns to the caddy and says, "I guess you'd better pick them up and I'll hit some more."

Sikes taps his driver against the turf. "This," he says, "is a frustrating game."

5:16 P.M.

Playing for position, not for distance, seeking to avoid the fairway bunkers on the left, Tommy Aaron hits a three-wood off the eighteenth tee. He avoids the bunkers, but pushes his shot off to the right and into the woods. He is forced to chip back onto the fairway. Then he strokes a five-iron to the green and two-putts for a bogey and a round of 74 that puts him in the clubhouse at 142, two under par.

Aaron admits that, after his 40 on the front nine, he is not too disheartened by his score or by his closing bogey. "I could have made a double-bogey," he says. "I've missed a lot of greens with a five-iron."

5:19 P.M.

Takaaki Kono comes to the eighteenth hole, needing only a par to finish with a 67 and win the crystal vase for low round of the day. He has already picked up seven birdies, including one on each of the par-five holes, even though he hasn't reached any of the par-fives with his second shot.

Kono hits a decent drive down the fairway, then knocks his approach shot at the flag. The ball lands just beyond the pin and rolls to the back fringe, some thirty feet from the hole.

His first putt goes four feet past the cup. Already, he has sunk half a dozen putts from this distance. But this time, Kono misses. He takes a bogey and moves to the scorer's tent with a 68, tying two considerably more famous golfers, Billy Casper and Gary Player, for low round of the day. He is, at 143, tied for seventh place, a much more lofty position than any other Asian golfer has ever held halfway through the Masters.

5:30 P.M.

Three men who have suffered through long days—Jack Nicklaus, with a 75; Grier Jones, with a 75; and Steve Melnyk, with a 76—are commiserating on the putting green. "Which one of us," says Melnyk slyly, "is going to shoot the 80 tomorrow?"

5:45 P.M.

Al Geiberger bogeys the eighteenth hole—to the great relief of Bob Rosburg, Vinnie Giles, Dale Douglass, Geiberger and Hsieh Yung-Yo. Geiberger's bogey gives him a round of 77 and a halfway score of 150.

Forty-two men have already finished with scores of 149 or better, and of the four players still on the course, only one, Dean Refram, has a chance to break 150. Even if he does, all the men at 150—Rosburg, Giles, Douglass and Yung-Yo—will place among the top forty-four plus ties and will be eligible to play the last thirty-six holes.

Geiberger comes up with a statistical note of his own. "Yesterday," he says, "I played with Tommy Aaron and he shot a 68, the lowest round of the day. Today, I played with Michael Bonallack, and he shot an 86, the highest round of the day."

Geiberger smiles. "For a while," he says, "I thought I was on my way to an 86 myself."

5:48 P.M.

In the interviewing room, Takaaki Kono, a smile splitting his face, is reviewing his round through an interpreter. He tells the reporters gathered in front of him that not one of his seven birdie putts was from more than eight feet away.

"Hey," one newspaperman yells to the interpreter. "Ask him what course he played today."

April 10, 1970

5:53 P.M.

Sukree Onsham walks off the eighteenth green, beaten by the Augusta National course. He comes in with an 84 for a thirty-six-hole total of 162. Only one man in the entire field has shot higher: Ralph Guldahl, who is fifty-seven years old.

Millions of television viewers will have no opportunity tomorrow to see the representative of the Land of the Smiling Thais.

6 P.M.

As they drive away from Augusta National, Billy Casper turns to his wife, Shirley. "I really want to win it," he says.

6:05 P.M.

Dan Sikes sips a vodka and tonic in the upstairs locker room. "The field here," he says, "just seems to ebb and flow like a great whale taking deep breaths. Guys get hot, then they have bad streaks. The pressure is tremendous, and you just don't get and keep the upper hand against this course for very long at a time."

6:15 P.M.

Dave Stockton, who is one of the playing editors of *Golf Digest*, phones his publisher and says that he would like to skip a small dinner party the magazine has scheduled. "Last year, I went out on Friday night," Stockton explains, "but I didn't honestly believe I could win the Masters. This year I really believe I can, and I'd prefer to stay at home and review the way I'm playing the course. Do you mind?"

The publisher doesn't mind. He wouldn't be at all upset if a member of his staff won the Masters.

7:05 P.M.

Gene Littler can't talk golf with Phil Rodgers tonight. Rodgers has missed the cut and is on his way out of Augusta.

7:15 P.M.

The defending champion, George Archer, who is at 145 after a par round, is having dinner at the home of an army colonel from Fort Gordon. Archer seems more interested in the colonel's World War II photographs than in worrying about the Masters.

"I'm just glad I made the cut," Archer says. "I have to stick around anyway and put the green coat on the new champion Sunday, so I'm glad I'm playing."

7:30 P.M.

Dave Stockton calls Augusta National from his rented home and finds that he is paired, for tomorrow, with the Japanese star, Takaaki Kono. "I guess it's my week for international relations," says Stockton.

8:45 P.M.

Bert Yancey is playing backgammon at the J. B. Masters home. Soon, he will turn on the yellow light.

9:30 P.M.

So far, there hasn't been even the slightest hint of a demonstration, but still, the Pinkertons are on duty outside Gary Player's rented home.

10:10 P.M.

In his room at Augusta National, Steve Melnyk is reading *The Greatest Game of All*, the autobiography of Jack Nicklaus. Melnyk is struck by the parallels between Nicklaus' career and his own. He notices that he and Nicklaus are the only two men ever to win the U.S. Amateur and the Western Amateur in the same year. He notices that both of them won major tournaments at the Oakmont Country Club outside Pittsburgh—Nicklaus the U.S. Open, he the U.S. Amateur. And Melnyk notices, too, that the first time Nicklaus played in the Masters, as an amateur, he failed to survive the cut. Melnyk has made the cut. Of course, he is twenty-three years old; Nicklaus made his first appearance at Augusta at the age of nineteen.

April 10, 1970

11:15 P.M.

Dave Stockton is in his living room, but he is not watching television tonight. He is reading a book called *Comeback*, the autobiography of Ken Venturi, who came so close to winning the Masters as an amateur fourteen years ago. Venturi went into his first Masters intending to win it, and birdied the first four holes. "Why should I be worried?" Stockton asks himself. "Look what being a little cocky did for him."

THE LEADERS AFTER THE SECOND ROUND

Bert Yancey	69-70—139
Gene Littler	69-70—139
Bob Lunn	70-70—140
Billy Casper	72-68—140
Tommy Aaron	68-74—142
Gary Player	74-68—142
Takaaki Kono	75-68—143
Dave Hill	73-70—143
Dave Stockton	72-72—144
Charlie Coody	70-74—144
Larry Hinson	72-72—144
George Knudson	73-72—145
R. H. Sikes	70-75—145
Orville Moody	73-72—145
Charles Coe	74-71—145
George Archer	73-72—145

SATURDAY

April 11, 1970

The Missionary Moves Up

F orty-eight men have survived the cut, and, as always, there are notable names among the missing. Roberto de Vicenzo, a stroke too high; Harold Henning, the winner of the par-three contest and one of the top twenty-four finishers in three of the past four years; Ray Floyd, the PGA champion; Lionel Hebert, after three straight years in the top ten; and Bob Goalby, the 1968 Masters champion, are a few of the casualties.

For the first time in many years, there are no startling surprises among the men who made the cut, no obscure amateurs and no ancient champions (Julius Boros and Sam Snead, despite their years, still swing too smoothly to be considered ancient). Probably the two most unlikely survivors are a pair of foreigners, Maurice Bembridge of England and Hsieh Yung-Yo of Nationalist China, each making his first Masters appearance.

Sixty per cent of the foreign professionals, nine out of fifteen, are still alive and two thirds of the American professionals, thirty-six of fifty-four. Only three of fourteen amateur entries remain in the competition: Steve Melnyk, Vinnie Giles and the perennial contender, forty-six-year-old Charles Coe, playing in his eighteenth Masters.

For the surviving players, there are now only two major

targets: Perhaps a dozen men are shooting for first place, and the rest are aiming for the top twenty-four. Any other target is insignificant now, in terms of prestige or of money.

The Masters is not a big-money tournament. Last year, George Archer collected $20,000 for winning; no official PGA tournament offered a smaller first prize. The title is worth far more than the purse. And, lower down in the rankings, the money is so evenly distributed that a few strokes' difference in score—which can mean thousands of dollars in some tournaments—means little in Augusta. The men who tied for thirteenth in 1969 earned $2,700 apiece. The man who came in forty-fourth, fifteen strokes further back, earned $1,450.

The Masters deliberately spreads its wealth: Every pro who tees off, whether he makes the cut or not, collects $1,000. Every professional honorary invitee who shows up, each former Open and PGA champion, even though he never lifts the club, collects $500.

The financial rewards of the Masters are so insignificant, relatively, that by design the amounts are never mentioned, either during the award ceremonies or on the national telecasts.

7:59 A.M.

The gates at Augusta National open, and Carol Martin, a twenty-two-year-old girl from Atlanta, heads immediately for the eighteenth green. She is carrying a folding golf seat and she wants a choice location, a perfect place to watch the golfers finish, a perfect place to be glimpsed by the television cameras.

This is the tenth straight year that Carol has staked out a spot by the eighteenth green. "I was once on the cover of *Sports Illustrated*," she says. "Along with the rest of the gallery around eighteen, of course."

She is with a friend from Augusta, Walter Howard, nineteen years old, who is also putting in his tenth year at the finishing hole. Carol and Walter expect to see at least fifty people they know, regulars, in the crowd around the green.

They have their lunches with them, and they are ready for a long wait: The first twosome doesn't tee off until 11:04 A.M. No player will approach the eighteenth green until some six and a half hours from now.

8:05 A.M.

A woman in her sixties, Emma Plunkett, a physical education teacher from Ponca City, Oklahoma, picks out a seat in the grandstand overlooking both the fifteenth green and the sixteenth tee. She settles down and starts reading an Augusta newspaper. A veteran spectator at the Masters, Mrs. Plunkett knows that she will have to wait more than five hours before she sees any golf action in front of her.

9:10 A.M.

Jack Nicklaus is lying in bed, reading *The Godfather*. He is almost to the end of the novel about the inner workings of the Mafia, and he has come to the decision that, perhaps, the pressure on the golf tour isn't quite as tough as he thought.

9:50 A.M.

The lower locker room is practically deserted. Bob Rosburg, who is paired with Dean Refram in the first twosome of the day, sits by his locker, showing a bare foot to Miller Barber. "I've got a ruptured blood vessel in the toe," Rosburg says. He puts on his golf shoes, takes a few steps, winces and shakes off the pain.

"I didn't think I'd make the cut," Rosburg says. "Now I'd like to make the top twenty-four. I've got to shoot my way back in."

He shakes his head. "It's a funny game," Rossy says. "I played a practice round here with Gene Littler the other day, and he was so unhappy with his game, he said he wanted to quit."

10 A.M.

Since he is not teeing off until after two o'clock, Billy Casper allows himself a modest breakfast of avocados and boiled shrimp.

His wife, Shirley, glances through the sports section of the local paper. "Did you see that Tommy Aaron started off bogey, par, bogey, double-bogey yesterday?" she asks.

Casper nods.

"His heart had to be in his stomach," says Shirley Casper.

"I know the feeling," says her husband.

10:04 A.M.

As Sam Snead enters the locker room, a reporter asks him about his playing partner yesterday, Takaaki Kono. "Shoo," says Snead, "did he get the ball in the hole! He had twelve oners. Twelve one-putts!"

The conversation turns to other Asian golfers, and Bob Rosburg mentions Chen Ching-Po, a Nationalist Chinese pro who placed among the top twenty-four in the 1963 and 1966 Masters. "The only thing that finally drove him off," says Rosburg, "was that he hurt his elbow tipping his hat to the crowd."

"Kono hit a long ball?" someone asks.

"Yeah," says Snead. "And if that sunovabitch weighs 140 pounds, like he says, he must be carrying lead in his pants."

10:10 A.M.

The Mysterious Mr. X, Miller Barber—he got his nickname when he first came on the tour, because his fellow pros never saw him at night—walks over to a representative of Izod, the company that makes the golf shirts with the alligator symbol. "You got any striped ones?" Barber asks.

"Hey, Miller," Bob Rosburg calls. "Didn't you hear? Stripes are out. You're gonna have to throw out your whole wardrobe."

10:15 A.M.

Daniel Field, the local private airport which usually accommodates two or three dozen planes, is now heavy with traffic.

April 11, 1970

More than two hundred private planes are expected to come in and out during the day.

Arnold Palmer's white jet, with red and blue stripes, is parked next to the terminal, an American flag on its tail. A sign hangs on the door to the terminal: NO GOLF SHOES.

10:18 A.M.

"Is there much of a crowd out at the practice tee?" Bob Rosburg asks.

"A few dozen people," someone says.

"The way I'm hitting," Rossy says, "I'll drive them away."

Rosburg hesitates. "I really don't want to go out there," he says. "My playing partner's the only one out hitting. I wish there were a few more so nobody would notice me."

10:39 A.M.

Sam Snead walks into the back of the pro shop. "Where can I find a hammer?" he asks. The manager of the shop hands him a hammer, and Snead begins pounding his putter with it. Despite his problems on the Augusta greens, he isn't trying to destroy the club, only to fix it.

10:41 A.M.

After twenty minutes on the practice tee, Bob Rosburg returns to the locker room. "I got way over at the end of the tee," he says, "and just aimed at the middle."

He picks up his putter. "Now I'll take this magic wand and see what I can do."

10:52 A.M.

Arnold Palmer strolls into the locker room, and the dozen reporters gathered there grow quiet, paying homage to the king. One of them brings up Palmer's political ambitions—he has been mentioned as a possible Republican candidate for governor of Pennsylvania—and suggests that Richard Nixon ought to appoint him to the Supreme Court.

Palmer laughs, dismissing the notion. "But I am getting an honorary doctor of laws degree from Wake Forest in two months," he says.

"You'd be as good as some of the judges on the Court now," a newspaperman says.

Palmer accepts the flattery without question. "I'll tell you," he says, "they ought to investigate some of those people. That Douglas!"

The sportswriters nod sympathetically. And Palmer then amuses them by telling two obscene jokes, one about two crows discussing a jet, the other about a spinster and a Chinaman.

All the reporters roar.

10:54 A.M.

Bob Rosburg walks over to the side of the putting green. "The other night," he says, "I was having dinner with Ray Floyd and Larry Ziegler—they both missed the cut—and Zieg said grace. I never heard anything like it. He said, 'Rub-a-dub-dub, thanks for the grub, yea, God!' "

10:59 A.M.

On the veranda outside the clubhouse, the wife of a professional golfer is telling about a conversation she overheard between Arnold Palmer and his wife, Winnie. "Arnold was talking about running for governor of Pennsylvania," she says, "and he turned to Winnie and said, 'Get me a book about politics. I know the difference between Democrats and Republicans, but I'm not sure about the other stuff.' "

"I hope she got him a book with a lot of pictures," purrs another golfer's wife.

11:05 A.M.

Tony Jacklin, relaxing on the veranda with his wife, Vivien, considers the question: Have you become as Americanized personally as you have as a golfer?

"When Viv and I came here the first time," Jacklin says,

April 11, 1970

"we looked at things and translated the price from dollars back to pounds. Now, when we go home to England, we count everything in dollars."

11:06 A.M.

Two women are standing by the first tee, studying the pairing sheets, trying to decide which twosome to follow for the day. "Let's follow Julius Boros," says Mrs. H. M. Sanderson of Marietta, Georgia. "He's so relaxed."

"No," argues Mrs. C. M. Grubbs of Rock Hill, South Carolina. "I want Chi Chi. He gives us a little show. He makes me feel appreciated."

11:42 A.M.

In the garage next to the J. B. Masters home, Bert Yancey, wearing tan Levis and a faded golf shirt, is leaning against an automobile, holding a pair of electric zoom binoculars and a pair of pliers. He is trying to repair the binoculars for his mother to use later in the day. Mr. and Mrs. Masters, and Yancey's wife, Linda, are standing outside the garage, and no one is saying a word.

Finally, Yancey looks up from the binoculars and breaks the silence. "I wish I could go fishing today," he says. "I really do."

11:44 A.M.

Steve Melnyk stands on the first tee. "I'm going for everything," he says. "I'm letting it all out."

He sinks an eighteen-foot putt to birdie the first hole, but he is still four-over for the tournament.

11:52 A.M.

Grier Jones and Bob Murphy, paired for the second time in three days, go off the first tee. They are playing under double pressure: For one thing, each needs a good round to get into contention for the top twenty-four. For another, they are playing right in front of Arnold Palmer.

"It's awful to be in front of Arnie's Army," says Gail Murphy, Bob's wife. "They're charging all over the place trying to get position to see Arnie's next shot while you're trying to play golf."

12:05 P.M.

As he awaits his tee-off time, Jimmy Wright stands by the practice green and measures the impact the Masters has had on him. "It's something like the awe of being in church, just being here," he says. "In church, you come in quiet, sit still, listen to the sermon, do what you're supposed to do, then get up and leave.

"We are on our good behavior here. When I drive up Magnolia Drive to the clubhouse, I see the sign that says '5 MPH.' I feel like if they found out I was doing 6 MPH, they'd send me off with my clubs and not let me play.

"At the PGA championship in Dayton last year, it seemed like the players owned the clubhouse. We talked loud, brought our guests right in to eat where we ate, and I suppose if I wanted to toss my shoes into the locker across the room, I could have. At Augusta, you just don't do that. You wouldn't think of doing that."

12:07 P.M.

Bert Yancey stretches out on the trunk of a car outside the J. B. Masters home, his eyes closed, deepening his suntan and thinking about Augusta National.

12:20 P.M.

The traffic is heavy as Bob Lunn drives from the Holiday Inn to the Augusta National Golf Club. Waiting for a chance to pull into the club, Lunn turns to his father, Axel. "If I can get by the first couple of holes," he says, "I'll be OK."

April 11, 1970

12:25 P.M.

Bert Yancey hasn't heard that stripes are out. He has changed into slacks and a blue-and-white, horizontally striped shirt. "Mother come yet?" he asks J. B. Masters.

"No," Masters says.

"When she does," Yancey says, "tell her I fixed the binoculars. All it needs now is a little battery."

Yancey turns and starts walking to the nearby course, and someone asks if he'd like a ride.

"No, thanks," Bert says. "I have a little ritual I go through every day with the cop at the gate."

12:26 P.M.

On the first hole, Frank Beard rolls in a three-foot putt for a birdie.

12:28 P.M.

George Archer stands on the practice range, talking, between shots, with a reporter. "What happens if you win again?" the reporter asks. "Do you put the green jacket on yourself?"

"I don't know," says Archer. "It doesn't seem too likely."

Archer looks up and sees Jack Nicklaus practicing next to him. "Say, why don't you ask Jack?" Archer suggests. "He's the only guy to win two in a row here."

The reporter walks over to Nicklaus and repeats the question. Nicklaus glances over at Archer, who has a quizzical, interested look on his face.

"You gotta put on your own coat," Nicklaus calls.

"You don't get any help?" says Archer.

"Nope," says Nicklaus. "No help."

After Nicklaus leaves the tee, Archer says to the reporter, "Jack always looks at me like I'm a little nutty. Oh, well, all I have to do is shoot two 65s and I can put on my own jacket."

12:32 P.M.

As Bert Yancey walks through the gate to Augusta National, the policeman on duty, Luke Williams, from the sheriff's office, shouts, "You don't come out on top today, I'll have you out here directing traffic tomorrow."

Yancey smiles and strides toward the clubhouse.

12:38 P.M.

On the second hole, Frank Beard rolls in a fifteen-foot putt for an eagle. In less than half an hour, he has moved from three-over to even-par, from a tie for twenty-eighth place into a tie for ninth.

12:45 P.M.

Billy Casper joins the clubhouse crowd, looking as serene as if he were in church. "Don't you ever get excited?" someone asks.

"No," says Casper. "If you're excited you use a lot of energy you could save for something else."

12:54 P.M.

"Hi, chappie," says Gary Player.

"Hi, laddie," says Billy Casper.

Player walks over to Casper, who is delivering a short interview-sermon to the press. Among other things Casper has revealed to reporters asking him about the pressures of the Masters is: "Seek not for riches, but for wisdom, and you shall gain riches and wisdom in eternal life." Casper, a missionary for the Church of Jesus Christ of Latter-Day Saints, can quote Scripture with considerable accuracy and believability.

"Nice round yesterday," says Player.

"You too," Casper responds.

The two of them walk over to a corner of the locker room and talk quietly for a few minutes. Then Player goes outside. "What was that all about?" a reporter asks Casper.

"I'd given Gary some books on the Mormon religion," Casper says, "and he thanked me for them and told me he'd read them and found them interesting and important."

April 11, 1970

Casper starts for the practice tee. "But I'm sure they're nothing Gary'd put into his life," he adds. "He's already got a great faith in his own Protestantism."

12:55 P.M.

On the fourth hole, Frank Beard rolls in a thirty-foot putt for a birdie. Now he is one-under and tied for seventh place.

1:15 P.M.

Glenda and Janice Weatherly, sisters from Augusta, walk past the clubhouse, both wearing a dozen or more large yellow-and-blue buttons inscribed: HILL'S ANGELS. Each is carrying a bagful of buttons and offering them to anyone who wants one.

"How'd you get to be a Dave Hill fan?" someone asks.

"Well," says Glenda, "I don't really know. We met a fellow who said he was Dave Hill's manager and he was a nice guy and he gave us all these buttons and, well, here we are."

1:20 P.M.

As Dave Stockton stands on the edge of the practice green, a sportswriter suggests to him that he should greet his playing partner, Takaaki Kono, with a bow. "It's a time-honored Japanese custom," the writer explains. "It'll help Kono feel at home."

"I guess it would be a nice gesture," Stockton says. "I'll do it."

1:21 P.M.

On the sixth hole, Frank Beard rolls in a twelve-foot putt for a birdie. Five-under for six holes, he is now two-under for the tournament, tied for fifth place and threatening the leaders. He is also threatening the Augusta National record for the front nine: 31, set by Craig Wood in 1940 and equaled by six players since then.

1:36 P.M.

Dave Stockton bows to Takaaki Kono. Kono returns the bow, then slams his drive more than 250 yards down the middle of the first fairway, outdistancing Stockton by a good ten yards.

Then, for his second shot, Kono takes a seven-iron. He lofts his shot toward the green, and the ball lands, takes two bounces and rolls into the cup for an eagle.

Kono takes off his white hat to acknowledge the cheers of the crowd and strolls cheerfully toward the green, as calm as if he scored eagles on Augusta National's par-four holes all the time. Actually, he only does it once a year. No one else has ever done it more than once in a lifetime.

Kono is now three-under for the tournament, and when a nine-year-old South Carolinian named Dave Chapman asks him for a souvenir, he gives away the ball with which he scored the eagle.

1:59 P.M.

On the second hole, after exchanging bows with Dave Stockton once again, Takaaki Kono picks up a birdie. "I think I can stop bowing to him now," Stockton says. "I don't think he could feel any more at home if he were in downtown Tokyo. I've got two pars, and he's got me feeling like I'm ten-over."

1:23 P.M.

Dave Stockton slips three new golf balls out of a package and puts them in his bag. He also tosses in a couple of boxes of raisins, energy food to fight off the fatigue that set in on the back nine yesterday.

1:35 P.M.

As Billy Casper comes off the practice tee, he stops to chat with a reporter he knows. He talks about his political and philosophical beliefs. He mentions that he has campaigned for both Ronald Reagan and Richard Nixon. "Athletes," he says, "have a great influence on every phase of man's life. And that is why

April 11, 1970

an athlete must conduct himself in an exemplary way, always."

Casper offers his opinion that "a balanced budget should be the number one thing in all our lives," and he adds, "A liberal element has crept into our schools. It has filtered down from the teachers. So now youth doesn't like to abide by rules and regulations."

As a final note, before he moves to the practice green, Casper says, "Parents do not take the time to love, guide and discipline the youth of America."

Then the millionaire missionary picks up his putter and goes to work.

2 P.M.

The current leaders:

PLAYER	HOLES	SCORE
Yancey	36	−5
Littler	36	−5
Casper	36	−4
Kono	38	−4
Lunn	36	−4
Beard	44	−2
Player	36	−2
Aaron	36	−2

2:01 P.M.

After pars on the seventh and eighth holes, Frank Beard bogeys the ninth and loses his chance to tie the course record for the front nine. He settles, without complaint, for a 32.

2:11 P.M.

On the veranda outside the clubhouse, John Jacobs, who is considered the best teaching pro in Europe, is analyzing the success of Takaaki Kono. "He's small," Jacobs says, "but this course is built for his game. Everybody misses greens here, and he's a terrific scrambler. He can get it up and down from anywhere. The Japanese are the best in the world at that."

2:13 P.M.

Apollo 13 lifts off from Cape Kennedy, heading toward the moon.

2:16 P.M.

On the second hole, Gary Player's second shot, a three-wood, rolls through a trap and onto the green, and the South African takes full advantage of the break. He makes a fifteen-foot putt for an eagle, at four under par, and bolts into the fight for the lead.

2:18 P.M.

Billy Casper comes out of the gate fast. On the first hole, he misses matching Kono's eagle by two inches. He taps in his birdie to move into a tie for the lead with his playing partner, Bert Yancey, and with his fellow Southern Californian, Gene Littler.

2:25 P.M.

As Dan Sikes watches his drive sail down the eleventh fairway, he says to his playing partner, Ken Still, "I hit a new ball, but it looks like it's wavering a little. I'd better change it first chance I get."

Then, on his approach shot, Sikes hits the ball into the stream guarding the green. "Adios!" he calls. "Seven years I've been playing here, and that's the first time I've hit a ball in that lake."

Sikes takes a double-bogey six that destroys a strong round and eliminates him from contention for the championship. "I was thinking about changing the damn ball instead of about planning the shot carefully," he says. "You've got to concentrate every second on this course. If you don't . . ." His voice trails off.

April 11, 1970

2:30 P.M.

The current leaders:

PLAYER	HOLES	SCORE
Yancey	37	—5
Casper	37	—5
Littler	38	—5
Lunn	38	—5
Aaron	39	—4
Player	39	—4
Kono	41	—4

2:32 P.M.

Bert Yancey birdies the second hole and becomes the first man all day to have first place to himself.

2:36 P.M.

Gene Littler's three-foot putt for a birdie on the third hole gives him a tie for the lead. Bob Lunn also birdies three.

2:39 P.M.

Tommy Aaron is through the first four holes—the holes he played in straight fives yesterday—and he has shot three, five, three, three, a pair of pars and a pair of birdies, boosting himself into contention.

3 P.M.

The current leaders:

PLAYER	HOLES	SCORE
Yancey	40	—6
Littler	41	—6
Casper	40	—5
Lunn	41	—5
Aaron	42	—4
Kono	44	—4
Player	42	—4

3:10 P.M.

Bert Yancey and Billy Casper bogey the fifth hole.

3:21 P.M.

Gene Littler's fifteen-foot putt for a birdie on the seventh hole puts him seven-under for the tournament. He is the second man to have the lead all alone.

3:22 P.M.

Steve Melynk marches off the eighteenth green with his first sub-par round—a 71, the result of three bogeys and four birdies. "I just wish I could've shot a 71 yesterday," he says.

3:28 P.M.

As he starts down the tenth fairway, Dave Stockton begins munching his supply of raisins. He has eight pars and a birdie so far, mostly because he has been scrambling well. He has sunk two putts of six feet and one of fifteen to preserve pars.

His Japanese playing partner, Takaaki Kono, is three-under for his round, four-under for the tournament.

3:29 P.M.

Thirty feet off the eighth green, Tommy Aaron chips in for an eagle to move five-under for the round and seven-under for the tournament, tying Gene Littler for the lead.

Aaron's partner, Gary Player, birdies the eighth and trails the leaders by two strokes.

3:30 P.M.

The current leaders:

PLAYER	HOLES	SCORE
Aaron	44	−7
Littler	43	−7
Yancey	42	−5
Player	44	−5
Lunn	43	−5
Kono	45	−4
Casper	42	−4

April 11, 1970

3:31 P.M.

Grier Jones and Bob Murphy troop off the eighteenth green, each with a 73, each five-over for the tournament, each knowing he needs a sensational final round to finish among the top twenty-four.

3:35 P.M.

Billy Casper and Bert Yancey both birdie the seventh hole.

3:36 P.M.

Gene Littler's one-foot putt for a birdie on the eighth hole puts him eight-under for the tournament, and alone, once more, in first place.

3:37 P.M.

As Arnold Palmer trudges toward the clubhouse, with a 74 that puts him six-over, far out of contention, a woman standing near the eighteenth green turns to her husband. "Some players have all the luck that's good," she says. "Arnie's got all the luck that's bad."

"He's been up around the top for ten or fifteen years," the husband says. "That's a long time."

"Yes," says the wife, "but I like to see my age group stay up there."

"What's that, twenty-six?" says the husband.

"Twenty-nine and holding, honey," says the wife.

3:41 P.M.

Tommy Aaron finishes the front nine with a 31, tying the Augusta National record.

3:44 P.M.

On the tenth hole, Charlie Coody hooks his second shot, misses the green, then chips in for a birdie, to go two-under for his round and the tournament.

3:50 P.M.

For the second straight day, Jimmy Wright needs to sink a tricky putt on the eighteenth green to break par. Yesterday, he missed a ten-footer. Today, he faces a seven-footer, lines it up and makes it. "I know breaking par in one round is meaningless in itself," Wright says, "but I'm happy about it. It means something to me to be able to say I broke par in the Masters."

3:52 P.M.

With a bogey on seventeen and a par on eighteen, Frank Beard sits in the scorer's tent, adding up a 68, putting him one-under for the tournament. "The playing conditions were ideal," Beard says. "The greens were holding beautifully. The overcast made depth perception better. And there was no wind at all. You're gonna see a lot of wonderful scores out there today."

3:53 P.M.

In the clubhouse, surrounded by reporters, Arnold Palmer has no funny stories to tell, only an unhappy story of his troubles on the course. "Every day," Palmer says, almost as if he is confessing, "you start out with the thought you're going to recover and get back in contention. My problem lately is that I get demoralized right off the bat.

"The first hole, I start with all the enthusiasm I can possibly muster and hit my second shot three and a half feet from the hole, and I never touch the cup with my putt. 'Aw, that's not so bad,' I tell myself. 'That can happen any old time, even if things are going right.'

"So the next hole, I hit it just off the edge in two, and I end up making a three-foot putt for a par—on a par-five hole.

"That kind of knocks me down. So then I try to hit the ball a little closer to the hole and, as a result, miss a shot here and there."

Palmer pauses. "A lot of people offer suggestions," he says. "Old Freddie McLeod said the other day I'm not hitting it with the reckless abandon of a few years ago. Well, that isn't quite

April 11, 1970

right, because today I hit it with all the reckless abandon I could, and that sunovabitch still didn't go any closer to the hole. The times I went by the hole today, I three-putted. After you do that a few times, you start coming up a little short."

"Could it be nerves?" someone has the nerve to ask.

"It could be," Palmer says. "But I don't think so."

3:55 P.M.

Slumped in front of his locker, Tony Jacklin is shaking his head, as if he can't believe his score of 70. "I never hit the ball better," he says, "not even in winning the British Open. I drove incredibly well. But I only made two decent putts, of seven feet and fifteen feet. I could have shot 66 and been in contention."

He is one-over for the tournament and still has a chance to become the first Englishman to place among the top twelve at Augusta.

3:56 P.M.

On the eleventh hole, Charlie Coody sinks a forty-five-foot putt for his second straight birdie. "They could just as easy have been a bogey and a par," says Coody. "I must be doing something right." It isn't his socks: They're white today.

4 P.M.

The current leaders:

PLAYER	HOLES	SCORE
Littler	46	−8
Aaron	46	−7
Yancey	45	−6
Casper	45	−5
Player	46	−5
Kono	48	−5
Lunn	46	−5

4:05 P.M.

On the twelfth hole, Charlie Coody sinks a five-foot putt for his third straight birdie.

4:06 P.M.

The fifteenth hole is no problem for Jack Nicklaus today. He booms out his drive, cracks a two-iron to the green and sinks a thirty-foot putt for an eagle. Finally, after an up-and-down round—two bogeys and three birdies—Nicklaus is at one-under for the tournament. If he can pick up a stroke on the last three holes, he may be in position to make a run for the championship tomorrow.

4:13 P.M.

Gene Littler, playing safe, deliberately hits his second shot to the right of the eleventh green, avoiding the water. But then he hits a poor chip and two-putts for his first bogey of the day.

4:18 P.M.

On the thirteenth hole, Charlie Coody reaches the green with a five-iron and two-putts from sixty feet for his fourth straight birdie, matching the 1967 performance of Ben Hogan, who birdied the same four holes in a row. Hogan went on to play the back nine in 30 strokes and come in with an eighteen-hole total of 66—at the age of fifty-four.

4:23 P.M.

Gene Littler lines up a two-foot putt for a par on the twelfth hole, measures it from all sides, strokes it and misses.

4:25 P.M.

Bert Yancey consults with his caddy on the twelfth tee. "A good nine or an easy eight?" Yancey asks.

"Just an easy nine," the caddy suggests.

Yancey hesitates, then reasons that his caddy's advice has

April 11, 1970

been consistently good on club selection. He takes the nine iron and hits it easy—too easy. The ball splashes into the water in front of the green.

Yancey takes a penalty stroke and drops a new ball. He studies the pin, which is near the front of the green, and decides to aim for the front edge in the hope that he'll get close enough to salvage his bogey.

He chips, too delicately, and falls short of the green. Yancey strokes his fourth shot four feet from the cup, then misses the putt and takes a crushing triple-bogey six. He plummets from a tie for the lead clear out of the top five.

"Now," Yancey tells himself, "you're gonna find out just how good a golfer you are."

4:29 P.M.

On the thirteenth hole, Tommy Aaron suffers his second straight bogey and slips to five-under, tied with his playing partner, Gary Player.

4:30 P.M.

The current leaders:

PLAYER	HOLES	SCORE
Littler	48	−6
Casper	48	−5
Player	49	−5
Aaron	49	−5
Lunn	48	−5
Coody	50	−5
Kono	50	−4

4:41 P.M.

With pars on the last three holes, Jack Nicklaus comes in with a 69. He realizes that, at one-under, he is going to be six or seven strokes off the lead, but he isn't completely disheartened. "I'll have to have a real good round to be in contention tomorrow," he says. "I've shot 64 here, and 65, and 66, and that's what I need tomorrow. If I shoot 65, I'll be eight-under, and 280 can win the Masters. Besides, if I got hot, somebody up front just might shoot a 75. There's always a little apple-swallowing on the last day."

4:42 P.M.

The Masters does not go on nationwide TV until five o'clock, but in the lower locker room, a couple of dozen players and reporters are watching a closed-circuit hookup provided by CBS. "This is great," says Tony Jacklin. "Watch out for the yips," Tom Weiskopf shouts at a putter on the screen.

4:43 P.M.

Gene Littler lines up a two-foot birdie putt on thirteen, measures it from all sides, strokes it and misses. After reaching the green in two, he has three-putted. "Well," says Littler, who is almost unbelievably even-tempered, "there's still a lot of holes left."

His playing partner, Bob Lunn, who dropped his second shot into the water, takes a bogey-six and slips to even-par for the day, four-under for the tournament.

4:44 P.M.

On the thirteenth fairway, Billy Casper studies his shot to the green. All week, he has been playing conservatively on both the thirteenth and fifteenth, laying up short of the water and pitching on, hoping to get close enough to sink a birdie putt.

But now he decides to abandon his cautious approach. He pulls out his four-wood and belts the shot some 245 yards. The ball comes to rest on the green, thirty feet from the cup. Casper two-putts for a birdie that moves him six-under.

His playing partner, Bert Yancey, bouncing back from the triple-bogey on twelve, also two-putts for a birdie and climbs back to four under par.

4:45 P.M.

A Masters official steps onto the eighteenth green and addresses the gallery. "In about fifteen minutes," he says, "we're

April 11, 1970

going on national television on CBS. We ask you to please pick up all papers and put your feet inside the ropes. Augusta National always wants to look good."

The spectators (a) applaud, (b) pick up all pieces of paper they can find and (c) tuck their feet behind the rope.

Now the crowd will look as good as the fairways, which have been sprayed a brighter green than they actually are. It was a rough winter, and without the spray, the nationwide CBS audience might see some brown patches on the fairways.

Augusta National always wants to look good.

4:46 P.M.

On the long fifteenth hole, the one that most players feared would be almost impossible to reach in two, Charlie Coody hits his longest drive of the week. He decides he can go for the green with a three-iron.

After his string of birdies, Coody is so charged up he slams the three-iron over the green, more than 215 yards away. "I just blanked the flag all the way," Coody says, "and I was too strong."

From in back of the green, Coody takes three strokes and settles for a par.

4:56 P.M.

His second straight birdie—this one on the fifteenth hole—brings Gary Player to seven-under for the tournament and shoots him into first place, the sixth man to hold or share the slippery lead during the past two-and-a-half-hour barrage of birdies and eagles.

4:58 P.M.

Takaaki Kono has cooled off. On the seventeenth hole, he takes his fourth five—and his third bogey—in five holes. He is now only two-under for the tournament.

4:59 P.M.

George Archer is in with a 75. He is four-over and he can stop worrying about having to put the new green jacket on himself.

5 P.M.

The current leaders:

PLAYER	HOLES	SCORE
Player	51	−7
Casper	50	−6
Littler	50	−6
Coody	52	−5
Aaron	51	−5
Yancey	50	−4
Hill	52	−3
Stockton	53	−3
Lunn	50	−3

5:10 P.M.

On the seventeenth hole—the spot where he fell out of first place in the 1969 Masters—Charlie Coody sinks a thirty-five-foot putt for a birdie to go six-under for his round and for the tournament.

5:11 P.M.

Shifting back to his conservative strategy, Billy Casper decides not to try for the fifteenth green on his second shot. Instead, he lays up short of the water, pitches to the green and sinks a fourteen-footer for his birdie. He draws even with Gary Player at seven-under. "I'm glad I didn't go for the green," he says.

Bert Yancey, bidding to move into contention again, also birdies the fifteenth.

5:12 P.M.

Orville Moody comes into the clubhouse, rubbing an ace bandage on his right wrist. "Got a cyst bothering me," Moody

April 11, 1970

says. "I had a cortisone shot this morning, and I had to wear this bandage. It kind of messed up my swing. Made me turn my left hand over more."

Moody looks unhappy. "What'd you shoot?" someone asks.

"Seventy-one," says Moody.

After opening rounds of 73 and 72, Moody is now at even-par for the tournament.

5:13 P.M.

Maurice Bembridge, a young British professional, walks into the lower locker room and looks up at the television screen. He sees Dave Hill lining up a chip shot from the fringe of the sixteenth green. "That's a very difficult shot Hill has there," says Bembridge.

Tony Jacklin spins around. "I don't think it's so hard, Maury," says Jacklin.

A British reporter chimes in, "I think it's easy. Tell you what, Maury. I'll give you a-thousand-to-one he makes it. OK?"

Bembridge hesitates.

On the screen, Hill chips the shot into the hole, and the announcer explains that viewers are seeing a replay of a shot Hill sank several minutes earlier.

5:15 P.M.

Dave Stockton completes a consistent round—fifteen pars and three birdies for a 69—and his partner, Takaaki Kono, completes an erratic one—one eagle, three birdies, four bogeys and ten pars for a 71. Stockton is three-under for the tournament, Kono two-under, the two best scores among the golfers who have completed play.

5:18 P.M.

After a bogey on fourteen and a birdie on fifteen, Bob Lunn bogeys the sixteenth hole. He is one-over for his round, three-under for the tournament. "You can always come back," Lunn tells himself. "You can always get hot."

The Masters

5:19 p.m.

For a change of pace, Dave Stockton decides that he isn't going fishing today. "I usually do it to unwind and forget golf for a while," he says, "but I'm playing too well right now. I'm afraid I'm too far back to win, but I'm going to take a run at it."

Stockton doesn't feel at all tired. "The raisins worked," he says.

5:20 p.m.

In the clubhouse, Tony Jacklin watches Billy Casper lining up a fifteen-foot putt for a birdie on the sixteenth hole. "Casper for the undisputed lead now," says Jacklin, exaggerating his own British accent, mimicking Henry Longhurst, the British golf expert who is reporting from the sixteenth hole for CBS.

5:21 p.m.

Billy Casper's bid for the birdie on sixteen rolls up to the hole and falls in. As the ball drops, Casper does a little sideways dance step in celebration. He is now eight-under and all by himself in first place.

5:22 p.m.

Gary Player and his caddy are both studying his birdie putt on the seventeenth. It is about a twelve-foot putt.

In the clubhouse, Bob Charles of New Zealand watches the South African and the caddy whispering to each other. "Careful, Gary," Charles shouts at the television screen, "he'll give you the wrong line."

Player putts, too strongly, and misses the birdie. "He looks just like me," Steve Melnyk says, "when I was little."

5:23 p.m.

On the seventeenth hole, Gene Littler strokes his second shot, an eight-iron, to within one foot of the cup. Then his playing partner, Bob Lunn, desperate now to stay alive, puts his second shot, a wedge, into a bunker guarding the green.

April 11, 1970

Lunn goes down into the bunker and sees that his ball is buried. He sets himself and swings. The ball flies up, hits the lip of the trap and rolls back into the sand. Again, Lunn sets himself. This time, he takes a softer swing, trying to loft the ball out close to the hole. Again, the ball catches the lip and rolls back. "Oh, no," Lunn says aloud. And then, to himself, he adds, "I can't win. I've lost the tournament."

On his third try out of the bunker, Lunn pops the ball within two feet of the cup and sinks the putt for a double-bogey that virtually kills his chances of winning the 1970 Masters championship.

5:24 P.M.

Charlie Coody bogeys the final hole and completes a round of 67, the lowest round of the day and of the 1970 Masters so far. At five-under, he is the leader among the men who have finished, two strokes ahead of his playing partner, Dave Hill, and Dave Stockton.

5:28 P.M.

"It's good, Gene," yells Tony Jacklin, watching the telecast, as Littler lines up his one-foot putt on seventeen. "Pick it up."

Littler taps the ball in for his first birdie since the eighth hole.

5:29 P.M.

Gary Player stands on the eighteenth tee, five-under for the round, seven-under for the tournament. He has five birdies and not a single bogey. He decides to play safe, to stay clear of the traps on the left, and takes a three-wood instead of his driver.

He pulls the ball to the left of the fairway, not in the traps, but in the rough. The shot is normally a five-iron, but Player figures that his ball will probably fly out of the high grass. He takes a six-iron and, to his surprise, hits it clean. The ball sails into a bunker guarding the right side of the green.

Player, often considered the most gifted trap player in golf, pops his ball out to within eight feet of the hole. But he misses the putt, takes a bogey and comes in with a 68, putting him at 210, six-under, giving him the lead in the clubhouse.

Tommy Aaron, with pars on the last five holes, comes in with a 69 and 211.

5:33 P.M.

In the press room, one newspaperman turns to another. "I just had a terrific interview with Kono," the first one says. "He told me why he does so well here."

"Yeah? Why?"

" 'In my country,' he told me," says the first reporter, " 'we have built twenty-three courses, each one an exact replica of Augusta National, a perfect copy of the fairways, the bunkers and the traps.' "

The newspaperman can't keep a straight face. " 'And we build them for less money, too,' Kono said."

5:40 P.M.

With pars on the closing hole, Gene Littler and Bob Lunn, who started the day one stroke apart, finish the day six strokes apart. Littler, after a 70, is at 209, seven-under. Lunn, after a 75, is at 215.

"I hit the ball better today," Littler says, "but still not great."

5:41 P.M.

After his drive on the eighteenth hole, Bert Yancey finds his view of the green obstructed by a television tower. He consults with Master officials for four or five minutes, is given permission to take a free drop to avoid the obstruction, then spends a few minutes calculating the best spot for his drop.

April 11, 1970

He holds the ball over his shoulder and releases it. The ball hits the ground and rolls into a good lie.

"Way to drop, Bert!" yells Tom Weiskopf, watching the telecast in the clubhouse.

"Great drop," echoes Tony Jacklin.

Weiskopf and Jacklin are among Yancey's closest friends on the professional golf tour.

5:55 P.M.

"I'd like to have parred the last hole," Gary Player is telling reporters. "I played as well as I possibly could and that would've made it a super round."

"You have any plans for tomorrow?" someone asks.

Player smiles. "I have two seconds here," he says, "and no one remembers them. I'm going to give it a go. I'm going to try to get a birdie at every hole. I don't think there is anything else here except winning."

5:57 P.M.

"I can win the Masters," says Tommy Aaron, "and maybe I will tomorrow. With it this close, anybody can win."

5:58 P.M.

Billy Casper and Bert Yancey finally complete their round, and Casper, with a 68, leads the Masters at 208, eight under par, a stroke in front of Gene Littler, two in front of Gary Player. Yancey, with a 72, is tied for fourth place with Tommy Aaron and Charlie Coody, three strokes back.

6:04 P.M.

Gene Littler has a distinct flair for stating the obvious. "There are a lot of holes to play," he says, assessing his chances.

No one can accuse Gene Littler of being dishonest—and no one will ever nominate him for Bartlett's.

The Masters

6:12 P.M.

In the interviewing room, Billy Casper looks at the assembled reporters and smiles. "It seems like I've been here before," he says, "but the cast was a little different."

Exactly a year ago, on the eve of the final round of the 1969 Masters, Casper, at 208, held a one-stroke lead—but the runner-up was George Archer, not Gene Littler. One thing hasn't changed: Charlie Coody was among the players three strokes behind.

Someone asks Casper if he has thought about his strategy for tomorrow. "It depends on the players behind me," Casper says. "I may have to resort to charging. I'll just have to wait and see. I'm not going to play too cautiously. I'm only one stroke ahead."

Casper, a good businessman, makes certain he tosses in a plug for the sporting goods company whose clubs he endorses. "As soon as I took those new clubs out of the crate," he says, pointedly mentioning the manufacturer by name, "I knew they'd be good."

He is asked if the memory of 1969 will haunt him. "If I were a betting man," says Casper, "I would bet I won't shoot a 40 the front nine tomorrow."

6:18 P.M.

A woman reporter walks up to Shirley Casper outside the press room. "Is it hard cooking for Billy Casper?" she asks.

"Not really," says Mrs. Casper.

Five years ago, Casper lost forty pounds, cutting down to 185, on a highly publicized diet which included ground bear in green peppers, reindeer patties, hippo gravy and antelope stew.

"Gee, I'd like to be able to lose weight like he has," the woman reporter says.

"It just takes discipline," says Shirley Casper.

6:20 P.M.

Charlie Coody calls his wife, Lynette, in Abilene. "You won some crystal today," he says.

(*166*)

April 11, 1970

6:22 P.M.

"How do you feel about the tournament now?" someone asks Bert Yancey.

"I'm glad it's not over," says Yancey, "and I'm sure Billy wishes it were."

6:50 P.M.

"If I could have just one wish now," Jimmy Wright says, as he prepares to go out for dinner with his wife, Joyce, and a few visiting members of his Long Island club, "it would be to come back here next year."

With eighteen holes to go, Wright, at 218, two over par, is tied for nineteenth place in the Masters. If he can hold his position, he will get his wish.

7:40 P.M.

Charlie Coody and ten Texans from Abilene are grilling two-and-a-half-inch-thick steaks at a rented Augusta home. Coody's visiting physicians have prescribed Butazolidin, an anti-inflammatory drug, to soothe his stiff back before the final round.

Butazolidin is famous in sports: It was administered to Dancer's Image before the horse won the 1968 Kentucky Derby; when traces were found in his system afterward, he was disqualified.

It is perfectly legal for Coody to take "bute" during the Masters. The only drawback is that he won't be allowed to run in the Kentucky Derby this year.

8:50 P.M.

David Stockton, Jr., the golfer's one-year-old son, reaches into his toy box and pulls out a scaled-down golf club. He begins wielding it enthusiastically, narrowly missing the leg of Al Geiberger. "Well," says David Stockton, Sr., "at least *he's* ready for the last round."

The Masters

THE LEADERS AFTER THE THIRD ROUND

Billy Casper	72-68-68—208
Gene Littler	69-70-70—209
Gary Player	74-68-68—210
Bert Yancey	69-70-72—211
Charles Coody	70-74-67—211
Tommy Aaron	68-74-69—211
Dave Stockton	72-72-69—213
Dave Hill	73-70-70—213
Takaaki Kono	75-68-71—214
Jack Nicklaus	71-75-69—215
Frank Beard	71-76-68—215
Larry Hinson	72-72-71—215
Bob Lunn	70-70-75—215
Bert Greene	75-71-70—216
Orville Moody	73-72-71—216
Tony Jacklin	73-74-70—217
Bob Charles	75-71-71—217
Charles Coe	74-71-72—217

SUNDAY

April 12, 1970

Two In, Two Out

The villains wander out on the Augusta National golf course at seven in the morning. One is John W. Fischer, Jr., the 1936 U.S. Amateur champion; another is Denny Shute, the 1933 British Open champion; and the third is a man named Julian Roberts. They are official pinsetters of the Masters, the men who decide exactly where each pin shall be placed on each green during each round. Their selections, almost invariably, turn brave men pale, and bold putters timid.

There is a theory that because the Augusta greens are so demanding, the pinsetters, more than wind or rain or any other single factor, determine whether the scores in the Masters run high or low, and, at least for any one round, the theory seems sound. Yesterday, most of the golfers agreed, the pin positions were relatively tame, and the scores ran better than they had in either of the first two rounds.

Clifford Roberts, the man who runs the Masters, has explained that, over a full seventy-two holes, the pinsetting does not have a great impact on scores. "We have four basic positions for the pin on each green," Roberts has said, "and we use the same four every year."

The catch is that the Masters, naturally enough, does not

use the same eighteen pin positions on the same day each year. They are juggled, hole by hole, and if, by chance or diabolical design, the pinsetters should nominate the toughest position on every hole on the same day, the scores unquestionably will soar.

Not that there are any easy pin positions at Augusta National. Every green seems to slope and sway in a variety of directions, and even the most kind-hearted pinsetter would have trouble picking a placement without a deceptive break.

Today, traditionally the day of the most demanding placements, most of the golfers will be shooting for the pins, some seeking birdies to bid for first place, some seeking birdies to bid for the top twenty-four.

The competitors will be bidding, too, for more money than the Masters has ever offered before. First-prize money has been boosted from $20,000 a year ago to $25,000, and even twenty-fourth-prize money has jumped from $1,800 to $2,000. The total purse, for the first time in Masters history, exceeds $200,000.

7 A.M.

Jesse Ross, a nineteen-year-old Augustan who caddies for Bert Yancey, is lying in bed, dreaming of birdies. Suddenly, his mother shakes him awake. "Get going and pray that he wins," she says.

There is no standard or formal caddy fee at the Masters—some golfers who last for only two rounds pay as little as $60 or $70, and the typical golfer who survives the cut but does not place high pays between $100 and $200—but if Yancey should win, Jesse Ross is guessing that he will receive at least $1,000, perhaps even $2,000.

8:15 A.M.

An advertisement in the Augusta Sunday paper invites visitors to attend early services at a local church and suggests:

April 12, 1970

WATCH THE MASTERS—WORSHIP THE MASTER. Only in Augusta in April does He get second billing.

8:15 A.M.

After attending services at the Mormon church in North Augusta, on the South Carolina side of the border, Billy Casper returns to his rented home and sits down to a breakfast of pompano and grapefruit.

His son Billy, who is thirteen, eats more like a Melnyk than a Casper. Young Billy puts away four eggs, two pork chops and half a pompano. "He's a real moose," says his father, a reformed moose.

9:10 A.M.

For a change, Steve Melnyk isn't hungry. He sits in the upper locker room, holding his throbbing head. "I was out kind of late with a date last night," he says. "Two o'clock, something like that. I thought maybe it'd loosen me up."

Melnyk rubs his head. "I feel like the guy in the commercial," he says, "you know, the one with the blahs."

9:55 A.M.

Not looking quite awake, Arnold Palmer enters the locker room and studies the half-dozen reporters who are sitting around, killing time by interviewing each other while they wait for the action to begin. "One good thing about shooting the way I've been shooting," Palmer says, with a grin, "You get to play early while the greens are still smooth."

9:56 A.M.

Beyond the practice green, between the ninth green and the eighteenth, Willie Peterson stands and looks over the course. Most of the year, he is a salads-and-dressing man at Oscar's Salt of the Sea restaurant in New York City. But, for one week each year, when the Masters is held, Willie Peterson, thirty-nine years old, born in Augusta, is Jack Nicklaus' caddy.

"I'm a three-time winner," he says. "Been with Nicklaus every year since he was an amateur."

Peterson studies the placement of the pin on the ninth green and commits it to memory. His man is seven strokes off the lead, but Willie is optimistic. "We get here in 32," he says, "we're in."

Willie looks at the pin on the eighteenth, then stares at the sky. "We want a little rain," he says. "That'll stop the other fellows from getting much roll on the ball. We don't get any roll, anyway. We hit the ball so high, we carry every yard we get."

10:15 A.M.

Grier Jones is about to enter the Augusta National clubhouse for the "first" time. He is reenacting his arrival for the benefit of the annual Masters movie, and he isn't too thrilled by his film debut. He has to tee off in less than an hour, he hasn't had any breakfast, he hasn't hit any practice shots and he knows that he's going to have to shoot a sub-par round to finish among the top twenty-four.

"Besides," says his wife, Jane, "they want him to kiss me on the cheek. He's having fits."

10:28 A.M.

The first person to tee off on the final day of the 1970 Masters is Mr. X, Miller Barber. He's earned this questionable honor by shooting rounds of 76, 73 and 77 for a total of 226. "Never thought I'd be playing the last round of the Masters," he says, "and not feeling any pressure at all."

Mr. X is in forty-seventh place. The worst that he can do is slip below his playing partner, Dean Refram, to forty-eighth.

Refram, incidentally, is in the first official twosome off the tee for the third time in four days, probably a record for the Masters.

April 12, 1970

10:30 A.M.

Jack Grant, an Augusta policeman, and Bob Gay, in charge of the fire-fighting equipment at Augusta National, discover that the Masters flag, hanging outside the clubhouse, is upside-down. They haul it down, then pull it back up the correct way.

10:37 A.M.

A year ago, George Knudson came within a stroke of the Masters championship, but now, as he strolls toward the first tee, the slender Canadian, who likes to wear dark glasses and his hair long, is fifteen strokes behind Billy Casper. "Just a walk in the country today, I'm afraid," he says.

10:39 A.M.

As he comes off the practice tee and heads toward the putting green, Vinnie Giles turns to his caddy. "Watch me," the amateur says. "I just split my britches. If it shows too much, I'll change 'em."

It shows too much. Giles darts into the clubhouse and changes from pale-yellow to bright-red slacks.

10:43 A.M.

George Archer, starting to pull on his golf shoes in the locker room, spots a cockroach running across the floor. Archer leaps up and begins beating a shoe against the floor. "Do you have a badge?" he yells at the roach. "Do you have a badge? No one admitted here without a badge!"

10:58 A.M.

In the clubhouse, Jane Jones and Gail Murphy wish each other good luck. At the end of the first round, Grier Jones was five strokes ahead of Bob Murphy, but now, going into the final eighteen holes, they are even at 221.

11:30 A.M.

Midway between the first tee and the practice green, fifteen-year-old Gary Newton, who is not quite five feet tall, the youngest and shortest member of the litter-removal crew at the Masters, stops picking up scrap paper and studies the pairing sheet. The young black Georgian wants to check the tee-off time for his favorite golfer: Gary Player of South Africa.

11:40 A.M.

Larry Hinson slips on his golf shoes, getting ready to move out to the practice tee. He hasn't quite resorted to plaids, but he is wearing a bright aqua shirt and a glittering gold sweater. After a 71 yesterday, the young Georgian is tied for tenth place. If he should move into contention today, he definitely will be noticed. His outfit will light up every color television screen.

11:43 A.M.

Near the first tee, a Pinkerton officer, Jesse Smith, turns to another Pinkerton. "A lady over there by the practice green," says Smith, "is wearing one of those see-through half-bra things, and I was looking at her so hard, I didn't even notice she was taking pictures."

Spectators are not allowed to bring cameras on the Augusta National course.

The other Pinkerton pivots and walks toward the practice green—to check out the camera, no doubt.

11:46 A.M.

Charlie Coody will never be able to match Billy Casper for exotic foods. For lunch in the lower locker room, Coody orders a cup of vegetable soup, and a bowl of peaches with ice cream. "I feel confident," he says. He must; he isn't wearing his red socks today.

11:53 A.M.

"As far as I'm concerned," says Dave Hill, over lunch, "this is just another tournament. I don't care if it's the Masters or anything else, I play the same way. Nothing compares to the thrill of hitting golf shots. That's it. That's all I want to do."

April 12, 1970

Hill is blunt and opinionated, a rare individual in a sport that tends to breed introverted, predictable conformity. "I don't care about major titles," he says. "I don't care about publicity. I don't care if anybody remembers me or not. When I die, they can throw me in a pine box and forget me."

Hill shakes his head. "I've got no real friends out here on the tour except Howie Johnson," he says. "We room together, and we go our own way."

Then Dave Hill, the second-leading money-winner on the 1969 pro tour, adjusts his eyeglasses, stuffs his cigarettes into his pocket and gets up to go to the practice tee.

11:58 A.M.

Jimmy Wright stands on the edge of the practice green. In a few minutes, he will be teeing off, and he knows almost exactly what he wants to do. At 218, two-over, he is tied for the nineteenth through twenty-fourth places in the tournament. To stay up there, Wright figures he needs a 73, perhaps a 72 if the scores run low.

"It's just about the only way a guy like me can come back next year," says the Long Island club pro. "I can't hope to get in the top eight of the PGA every year."

12:43 P.M.

Dave Stockton stops practicing his putting for a moment, stands back and studies the scoreboard. He sees, as he already knows, that he and his playing partner, Dave Hill, are tied for seventh place, five strokes behind Billy Casper.

He does not expect to win. He doubts that Casper will fade again, and he realizes that Gary Player, in third place, is probably the fiercest competitor in golf. But Stockton reasons that if he can match his round of yesterday, a 69, he will surely finish among the top five, perhaps among the top three.

He is pleased with his pairing. Hill is an excitable personality, and an intense player, and the combination has always stimulated Stockton when the two have played together in the past. "Just keep concentrating," Stockton tells himself. "Just don't make any mistakes."

12:48 P.M.

On the sixth green, for the third hole in a row, Chi Chi Rodriguez lags an approach putt up short of the cup. He is far out of contention, but nothing dampens his showmanship. Chi Chi turns to the gallery. "Hey," he says, "I'm only twelve strokes behind the leader, and I'm playing safe."

12:51 P.M.

His drive on the seventh hole hooks deep into the woods, his second shot strikes a tree, his third shot reaches the green, and then Steve Melynk three-putts for a double-bogey. He started the day three strokes behind Charles Coe in the contest for low amateur, and now he is five strokes back and his hopes are ruined. "I can't concentrate," Melynk says. "My head feels like a watermelon."

12:53 P.M.

As Grier Jones bogeys the tenth hole, to slip three over par for the day, hopelessly out of the battle for the top twenty-four, his wife grimaces. "Maybe I'd better take a separate plane out of here," Jane Jones says.

1:03 P.M.

Gene Littler strokes a putt on the practice green and steps back and watches it fall without emotion. "I'll do nothing different today than any other day," he says. "I'll just tee it up and try to play my game. I'll know how Billy and the others are doing from the scoreboard, and I'll try not to let it affect me."

1:09 P.M.

After rifling a two-iron nearly 250 yards to the second green, Jack Nicklaus strokes in a thirty-foot putt for an eagle. He vaults into a tie for seventh place at three-under, and the six

April 12, 1970

men in front of him, all standing around the practice green, hear the roar from the second green and know that Nicklaus has begun his move.

1:17 P.M.

On the putting green, Gary Player starts taking a few practice swings, shadow swings without a club in his hand. Something doesn't feel quite right to him. He leans over, removes his right shoe and pulls off a sock, exposing another sock. Then he takes off his left shoe, slips the extra sock over the sock on the left foot, then puts both shoes back on and laces them up. He swings a few more times and smiles. Now he feels balanced.

1:18. P.M.

Miller Barber rolls in a fourteen-foot putt for a birdie on eighteen to complete a round of 65—by two strokes the lowest round so far of the 1970 Masters, eight strokes lower than his best previous round of the tournament.

With his fantastic finish—on the back nine, he has fired a record-tying 30—Barber winds up at 291, probably in the top twenty-four, a lofty level that seemed unattainable only three hours earlier.

Mr. X credits his sudden improvement to a putting lesson from George Low, another mysterious Mr. X, a fellow in his sixties who travels the golf tour, giving occasional putting lessons and generally enjoying himself. Some people call George Low, who never played the tour regularly, the greatest putter in golf history. He calls himself America's guest.

"I started stroking with my arms instead of with my hands," says Miller Barber. "I had twenty-eight putts today. That's the difference."

1:25 P.M.

As he steps to the eighteenth tee, four-under for his round, four-over for the tournament, Bruce Devlin knows he needs a birdie or, at worst, a par to make the top twenty-four. He takes a double-bogey and goes to the clubhouse with a 70 and 294. "I'm going home," he says, thoroughly disappointed with his play. "I will not even bother to play at New Orleans next week. It would just be a waste of time."

Devlin has one small consolation: In each of his four rounds, he parred the treacherous eleventh hole, the hole that once cost him a green jacket.

1:26 P.M.

Tommy Aaron catches a bunker with his approach shot on the first hole and takes a bogey to slip four strokes behind Billy Casper.

1:41 P.M.

On the third hole, with his second straight birdie, Dave Stockton moves to five-under, within three shots of Billy Casper. Suddenly, Stockton realizes that if he can pick up another birdie or two on the front nine, he can actually win the Masters. The thought sends a chill sweeping through him.

1:48 P.M.

Bert Yancey guides a four-foot putt into the cup for a birdie on the second hole and climbs within two shots of Billy Casper.

1:55 P.M.

On the sixth hole, Jack Nicklaus raps a ten-footer into the cup for a birdie and, at four-under, edges within four strokes of Billy Casper.

1:56 P.M.

As Jimmy Wright steps to the tenth tee, Arnold Palmer is coming up the parallel eighteenth fairway. On the eighteenth green, not much more than one hundred feet from the tenth tee, an announcer booms out Palmer's biography to the huge gallery. He recites Palmer's championships, his money earnings, his brilliant record in the Masters.

April 12, 1970

Wright, half-listening to the announcement, slams his drive into the trees bordering the left side of the tenth fairway. He hits back to the fairway, wedges to the green, then three-putts for a double bogey six. On top of bogeys on the sixth and seventh holes, Wright sees his chances of placing among the top twenty-four slipping away.

"I swear that guy took ten minutes giving Palmer's life history," he says. "I shouldn't have let it get to me, but I did."

1:59 P.M.

Bert Yancey strokes an eight-foot putt into the cup for a birdie on the third hole.

2 P.M.

The current leaders:

PLAYER	HOLES	SCORE
Casper	56	−8
Yancey	57	−7
Littler	57	−7
Player	56	−6
Stockton	58	−5

2:04 P.M.

For the fourth straight round, Arnold Palmer fails to match par at Augusta National. He comes in with a 73 and a total of 295. It is the first time in fourteen years that Palmer has not shot at least one round of par or better in the Masters; even in 1968, the year he missed the cut, one of his rounds was a 72.

Strangely, Palmer's scorecard shows that, for the entire tournament, he played the first twelve holes in even par. "I've always felt," he says, "that if I could get past the first twelve holes in par or better, with those two par-fives coming up, I'd do all right." But Palmer's scorecard shows that, in the 1970 Masters, he played the last six holes in seven strokes worse than par.

"Do you think you have a chance ever to win here again?" someone asks.

"I'd like to think my chances are damn good for the next five years," says the forty-year-old Palmer. "At least."

2:17 P.M.

Jack Nicklaus has hit a big drive on the eighth hole, the hole that ruined him Friday. He decides to go for the green with a one-iron. He swings into the shot perfectly, but, on its way toward the target, the ball catches a branch of a tree, ruining Nicklaus' bid for an eagle. His shot stops at the edge of the green, and Nicklaus three-putts for a par.

2:18 P.M.

On the fourth hole, Billy Casper and Gary Player, paired in the final twosome of the day, each picks up a birdie-two. At nine-under, Casper moves two strokes in front, and Player shares second with Bert Yancey and Gene Littler.

2:23 P.M.

On the fifth hole, Bert Yancey and Gene Littler, paired in the next-to-last twosome of the day, each pick up a birdie-three and climb within a stroke of Billy Casper.

2:29 P.M.

Gary Player bogeys the fifth hole and slips three strokes out of the lead.

2:30 P.M.

The current leaders:

PLAYER	HOLES	SCORE
Casper	59	−9
Yancey	59	−8
Littler	59	−8
Player	59	−6
Stockton	60	−5

April 12, 1970

2:31 P.M.

Needing a birdie on the ninth hole to make the turn in 32—the target his caddy, Willie Peterson, set for him—Jack Nicklaus instead picks up a bogey and makes the turn in 34, three-under for the tournament. Only a miraculous back nine, something like Miller Barber's 30, can give Nicklaus a shot at his fourth Masters championship.

2:34 P.M.

Grier Jones, who began the 1970 Masters with a birdie and bright hopes, finishes with a bogey and no hope of penetrating the top twenty-four. His closing 75 gives him a total of 296. "I couldn't hit a shot," he says.

2:35 P.M.

Mrs. Evelyn Burns and Mrs. Mattie Hamilton, two black women, are washing their laundry at Taylor's Coin-Operated Dry Cleaning and Laundry in the National Hills shopping center, which faces Augusta National. A man walks in and asks, "Who's leading in the tournament?"

"What tournament?" says Mrs. Burns.

2:41 P.M.

This is not the day for miracles for Jack Nicklaus. He three-putts for a bogey on the tenth hole. "I'm out," he concedes.

2:42 P.M.

Bob Murphy, who began the 1970 Masters with a 78, finishes with a 71 and, at 292, has a chance to place among the top twenty-four for the first time in four appearances at Augusta.

2:49 P.M.

Sam Snead walks into the clubhouse after a round of 72. He has played the final fifty-four holes of the Masters in even par, which is not at all bad for a man of fifty-seven. In fact, if you deducted each man's age from his total score in the 1970

Masters, Sam Snead (292 minus 57=235) would be the new champion. In order to beat Snead on this basis, Billy Casper, who is thirty-eight, would have to shoot 272; Gene Littler, thirty-nine, would have to shoot 273; Gary Player, thirty-four, would have to shoot 268; and Larry Hinson, twenty-four, would have to shoot 258.

"Were the pin placements tough today!" Snead says to a reporter. "Whew! Man, only way they could have made it tougher would have been to cover 'em up and tell us, 'Go hunt 'em, boys!'"

2:50 P.M.

The 1967 Masters champion, Gay Brewer, sits in the locker room, packing to leave. He doesn't like the way he played—a closing 74 for 294—but, at least, he has something to show for the week: Six crystal goblets, his reward for scoring three eagles.

Brewer picked up an eagle and two goblets during each of his rounds, except the second. Curiously, the only time he broke par for the eighteen holes was the second round.

2:51 P.M.

Tony Jacklin stomps off the twelfth green, frustrated by Augusta National. He wants very much to do better than any Englishman in Masters history, but after taking a bogey on eleven and a double-bogey on twelve, he is two-over for the day and three-over for the tournament. Unless he makes a dramatic move, he will not finish among the top twelve. "There is no tougher course than Augusta," he says, "when your game starts to go."

2:52 P.M.

Dave Stockton lines up a twelve-foot putt for a birdie on the ninth green. He strokes it perfectly, straight for the cup, but just an inch too soon, the ball dies. Stockton slaps his hands against his knees and drops his head in frustration.

Eight times on the front nine, he has had putts of fifteen feet or less for birdies, but only twice has he sunk them. He taps

April 12, 1970

in his sixth straight par and moves to the tenth tee five-under for the tournament, even with his playing companion, Dave Hill, who has birdied two of the last three holes.

2:53 P.M.

Nursing a one-stroke lead, Billy Casper steps to the tee on the eighth hole, the hole that crushed Jack Nicklaus. He takes his driver, hoping for a chance to reach the green in two, and swings and pushes the ball out to the right. The shot lands in a fairway bunker.

2:56 P.M.

Gene Littler birdies the eighth hole to move to nine-under, tied for the lead.

2:57 P.M.

Billy Casper plays safely out of the fairway bunker on eight, but he is still far short of the green. A hill blocks his view of the flag. He walks up the hill, studies the shot, then moves back to his ball. He hesitates before choosing a club, strides up the hill once more, re-examines the shot and returns to his ball. He decides to hit a five-iron.

Casper gets eager with the five-iron and hooks the shot. The ball veers into the pines on the left of the fairway, rattles around and finally comes to rest on a roadway, against a curbing, between the eighth and second fairways, not far from a refreshment stand. Casper marches up to the ball, anxiously pinching his cheek, and, uncertain about the Augusta ground rules, asks a Masters official if he gets a free lift off the roadway. The official says no. Casper turns to another official and repeats his question. He is told he can move his ball away from the curb, but he must drop it on the roadway. He is lying three and he still is not on the green.

2:58 P.M.

Tommy Aaron birdies the ninth hole, his third birdie in a row and challenges the leaders at five-under. Aaron is now five strokes ahead of Charlie Coody, his playing partner. Coody, who lost last year because he gave up three strokes to par on the final three holes, isn't going to have to worry about pressure at the finish this year. He has already surrendered three strokes to par today and has disappeared from contention.

2:59 P.M.

After two double-bogeys, four bogeys and three birdies, Steve Melnyk signs his scorecard for a 77 and 297. He is not even going to be second-low amateur to Charlie Coe. His roommate, Vinnie Giles, came in earlier at 296.

As Melnyk walks dejectedly toward the clubhouse, a group of youngsters start asking him for golf balls. "I'm sorry," he says, in a tired voice, "I don't get those free like the other fellows."

Then he writes his caddy a check for $140 for the week. "When you're an amateur," Melnyk says, "you feel that."

He goes inside and sits down at the bar. "I just played rancidly," he says. "I was awful."

Melnyk pauses. "Damn," he says, "I can play this course. I hit a five-iron to the fifteenth today. Damn."

Then, shaking off the memory of the round, Melnyk brightens slightly. "It was an honor to play here," he says. "It's a fabulous tournament. And I'll be back next year. I'll still be qualified as the 1969 amateur champion, and I'll be back, and I'm going to do better. I know it."

3 P.M.

The current leaders:

PLAYER	HOLES	SCORE
Littler	62	−9
Casper	61	−9
Yancey	62	−8
Player	61	−6
Hill	63	−5
Stockton	63	−5
Aaron	63	−5

April 12, 1970

3:02 P.M.

The first time Billy Casper drops his ball on the roadway, it rolls immediately against the curb. The second time, the ball bounces far down the road, then comes to rest against the curb once more. Spectators are laughing, a little nervously; Casper is not. "Where's the ball?" he says.

"It's coming down," someone says.

The ball is passed back up the road, from a spectator to a cop to a rules official to Casper. Finally, unable to drop the ball into a playable lie, he is allowed to place it on a pile of wood chips in the roadway.

His fourth shot skims a branch and comes up short of the green. And then, with his fifth shot on the par-five hole, Casper reaches the green. He knows that he is about to tumble out of first place for the first time all day.

3:05 P.M.

Dave Hill birdies the tenth hole, his third birdie in four holes, and moves six under par, one stroke ahead of his playing partner, Dave Stockton, and within striking range of the leaders. "This is just another tournament," Hill tells himself.

3:06 P.M.

On the eighteenth hole, with the pin placed toward the front of the green, Chi Chi Rodriguez fires his second shot almost all the way to the back, some sixty feet from the cup.

Chi Chi lines up his long putt and turns to the gallery. "When the hole is back here," he says, "I'm down there. When the hole is down there, I'm up here."

Chi Chi grins. "I'm too strong," he says. "Arnie Rodriguez. Puerto Rican power." This is the last hole, so he is using all his lines.

"C'mon, Chi Chi," someone in the crowd calls, "stop fooling around and putt the ball."

Rodriguez stops and stares at the spectator. "If you don't mind, sir," Chi Chi says. "This is my show."

Then he putts, and the ball curls across the undulating green, dips from the higher back level to the lower front level, rolls to the cup and falls in. The crowd bursts into applause, and Chi Chi bows deeply. "Chi Chi power," he explains.

Then, after his playing partner putts out, Chi Chi collapses on the ground, spread-eagled, as if he has fainted from the sight of his genius. He's earned a rest: He's posted a 68, the second lowest round of the day, and a total of 287, one-under for the tournament. Chi Chi is the first sub-par finisher in the 1970 Masters.

3:08 P.M.

Tony Jacklin birdies the thirteenth hole.

3:09 P.M.

With two putts, Billy Casper takes a double-bogey seven on the eighth hole, raising visions in his mind and in the minds of thousands of spectators of his collapse on the front nine a year ago.

Suddenly, Casper, at seven-under, is in third place, a stroke behind Bert Yancey and two behind Gene Littler.

3:10 P.M.

On the ninth hole, Gene Littler bogeys, and Bert Yancey pars, and the two of them move to the tenth tee, sharing the lead at eight-under.

3:18 P.M.

Tony Jacklin birdies the fourteenth hole.

3:19 P.M.

As bold with his shots as with his words, Dave Hill decides to go for the flag on the eleventh green, go for the birdie that can rocket him within a stroke of the lead.

Hill has enough courage, but his shot doesn't have enough carry, and he splashes into the stream protecting the green. He

April 12, 1970

chips on and sinks his putt for a bogey, slipping three shots off the pace.

3:20 P.M.

A jet roars over Augusta National, dips one wing in salute, and then Arnold Palmer turns and heads north to home.

3:21 P.M.

With the pressure on, Billy Casper delicately strokes a twenty-foot downhill putt into the cup for a birdie-three on the ninth hole. Now he is eight-under, in a three-way tie for first place with Bert Yancey and Gene Littler.

Gary Player follows Casper's example and rams in his birdie putt to climb within a stroke of the leaders.

3:27 P.M.

Playing the eleventh hole right behind Dave Hill and Dave Stockton, Tommy Aaron produces his fourth birdie in five holes and moves to six under par, only two strokes behind the leaders. "I've got a good shot at it," Aaron tells himself.

3:30 P.M.

The current leaders:

PLAYER	HOLES	SCORE
Yancey	64	—8
Littler	64	—8
Casper	63	—8
Player	63	—7
Aaron	65	—6
Stockton	65	—5
Hill	65	—5

3:31 P.M.

On the twelfth hole, in their own private battle, Dave Hill once again surges in front of Dave Stockton. Hill birdies to go six-under, and Stockton bogeys to go four-under.

3:32 P.M.

Tony Jacklin birdies the fifteenth hole. His third straight birdie puts him one-under for the day and even-par for the tournament—just the dramatic spurt he needed to carry him toward the top twelve.

3:40 P.M.

With a par on the final hole, Jimmy Wright finishes a round of 75, leaving him at 293 for the tournament, five over par.

He goes into the scorer's tent, adds up his card and learns that, of the twenty-six golfers who have finished play, eight have scores of 292 or lower. Twenty-two men are still on the course, and since fifteen of those men started the day at even-par or better, all the rest at two-over or better, Wright calculates that his chances of making the top twenty-four are practically nil. As he emerges from the tent, Wright spots a friend and signals him, with both hands, thumbs-down. "I kicked it away," Wright says. "I won't make it. I'll miss by one shot."

In twenty-nine of the thirty-three previous Masters tournaments, a score of 293 would have been good enough to make the top twenty-four.

3:43 P.M.

Dave Stockton closes the gap between himself and his playing partner to one stroke as he birdies the thirteenth and Hill three-putts from thirty-five feet for a par.

3:44 P.M.

On the eleventh hole, shying away from the stream, Billy Casper plays for the right-hand side of the green. He strokes a five-iron and goes too far, leaving a trap between his ball and the green. "I should've hit a six," Casper tells himself. "I just went to sleep. I forgot it was downwind."

3:47 P.M.

One year ago, Tom Weiskopf bogeyed the seventeenth hole and missed tying George Archer for first place by one

April 12, 1970

stroke. Now he comes off the eighteenth green two strokes ahead of Archer. But Archer is in with a 75 for 294, and Weiskopf has a 74 for 292.

"All I wanted to do today," says Weiskopf, "was make the top twenty-four."

Apparently, he has. Only four men have finished with scores better than 292, and unless all twenty men still on the course beat him out—which is possible, but unlikely—Weiskopf has won a return trip in 1971.

3:50 P.M.

After a weak chip, a concession to the pin placement dangerously near the water, Billy Casper two-putts and takes a bogey on eleven. He drops out of a tie for the lead and into a tie for third with Gary Player.

3:56 P.M.

The two Daves are even again, both at six-under, after Stockton birdies the fourteenth and Hill settles for a par. The traffic jam is almost unbelievable now—seven men within a two-stroke spread, each thinking how nice it would be to end the day in a green jacket. Only one of the seven contenders—Gary Player—already knows how he looks in official green.

3:57 P.M.

After twelve pars and two birdies, Frank Beard hits his second shot on the fifteenth hole into the water guarding the green. His bid to finish among the top five sinks with his Titleist. Beard bogeys the hole and is now two-under for the tournament.

3:58 P.M.

Charles R. Coe, the forty-six-year-old oilman from Oklahoma City, who doesn't play golf very often, comes in with a 75 and 292, clinching the gold medal, gold-and-silver cup and silver cigarette box awarded the low amateur in the Masters. He finishes two strokes ahead of Vinnie Giles, three ahead of Steve Melnyk.

Coe's remarkable performance strengthens a theory, widely held, that if he had decided to devote himself entirely to the game, he might have become one of the greatest golfers who ever lived, possibly even the greatest.

The Masters is only the second tournament Coe has entered in four years. He played in the 1969 U.S. Amateur and barely finished among the top eight to qualify for the Masters.

Between 1949 and 1966, Coe played in seventeen of eighteen Masters tournaments, once tied Arnold Palmer for second place, eight times finished among the top twenty-four, and five times came in low amateur in the tournament. He won the U. S. Amateur for the first time twenty-two years ago, then won again in 1958.

These days, he rarely plays golf more than once a week. "About ninety per cent of the golf I play is right here," says Coe, who is a member of Augusta National, "I play for personal satisfaction. If I can shoot well, that's a bonus."

Coe has an extra bonus: He has earned an invitation to his nineteenth Masters in 1971. Seven players are in at 291 or better, and even if all sixteen men on the course shoot 291 or better, the 292s, including Coe, will still rank among the top twenty-four plus ties.

3:59 P.M.

Jimmy Wright sits in the clubhouse, staring at his shoes, looking too drained to slip them off. He knows for certain now that 293 will not make the top twenty-four, that he will miss by a single stroke. "I feel empty," he says. "I wanted it so bad."

His playing partner, Deane Beman, who shot a 74 and finished at 292, walks in. "Sorry, Jim," says Beman. "It might have helped if I hadn't hacked it around so bad."

Wright appreciates Beman's attempt to console him. "Well," says Wright, standing up, "it's not the end of the world, I guess. But I sure wish we were having champagne now."

April 12, 1970

In a couple of weeks, Jimmy Wright will report back to the Inwood Country Club to begin the 1970 season as the resident pro.

4 P.M.

The current leaders:

PLAYER	HOLES	SCORE
Yancey	66	−8
Littler	66	−8
Player	65	−7
Casper	65	−7
Stockton	68	−6
Hill	68	−6
Aaron	67	−6

4:01 P.M.

On the twelfth hole, the hole where he once made what he calls the greatest shot of his life, Gary Player comes up with a pretty good one: A twenty-foot birdie putt that lifts him into a three-way tie for the lead at eight-under.

Billy Casper settles for a par, and now all three of the men who started the day as his challengers have stormed past him.

4:03 P.M.

As Tony Jacklin signs his scorecard for a 71 and even-par 288, a Masters official tells him that he'll probably be among the top twelve. The only man who has finished with a score lower than 288 is Chi Chi Rodriguez, and of the fourteen men out on the course, only ten are now under par.

4:04 P.M.

Tommy Aaron's bid to end his bridesmaid's role collapses on the fourteenth hole. He takes a bogey and, at five-under, falls three strokes behind the front-running threesome.

4:05 P.M.

Gene Littler and Bert Yancey both put their third shots on the thirteenth hole within five feet of the pin. Littler putts first, his putt finds the hole, and he goes into first place alone at nine-under.

4:06 P.M.

Dave Stockton and Dave Hill stand in the fifteenth fairway, each knowing that he must birdie this par-five hole if he wants to win the 1970 Masters championship. Both have hit good drives, and now both elect to go for the green.

Both carry the water, but neither holds the green. Stockton's two-iron shot, swept along by a trailing wind, is so strong that he almost reaches the pond in front of the sixteenth green, well beyond the fifteenth. His view obstructed by a tree, the pin set treacherously on the front of the green, on a downhill slope, Stockton chips past the pin, to the front fringe. Only a fine second chip enables him to preserve a par.

Hill two-putts for a par, and both men leave the fifteenth green at six-under, knowing that, barring a miracle, barring collapse on the part of all the leaders, they have lost their bids for the title.

The 1970 Masters has narrowed down to a four-way battle.

4:07 P.M.

Now Bert Yancey faces his birdie putt on thirteen. He is no more than four feet from the cup, perhaps three. He measures the shot carefully, studies the grain of the green, steps up and strokes the ball. He misses and remains at eight-under.

4:08 P.M.

Billy Casper does not like his lie, but he has no choice. He cannot play conservatively now. He takes out his four-wood and aims for the thirteenth green. The club connects, and the ball soars over the water and comes to rest safely on the putting surface, some forty feet from the cup.

April 12, 1970

Casper's playing partner, Gary Player, also reaches the green in two, approximately the same distance from the hole.

4:13 P.M.

Bidding for a birdie that will gain him a tie for the lead, Bert Yancey strokes a five-iron to within six feet of the cup on the fourteenth hole. "That," says Yancey, marching happily toward the green, "is the greatest shot of my life."

4:14 P.M.

Jack Nicklaus pars the final hole and, after birdies at fifteen and seventeen, posts a 69. At 284, he is the leader in the clubhouse, but he knows that his lead will be short-lived.

He is not even going to stick around to find out how high he finishes. "I'll be at the airport in half an hour," he says, "and I'll be home in Palm Beach an hour and a half later."

His only immediate plan is to finish reading *The Godfather*.

4:15 P.M.

With two putts, Gary Player birdies the thirteenth hole and goes nine-under, tying Gene Littler for first place.

4:16 P.M.

With two putts, Billy Casper birdies the thirteenth hole and goes eight-under, tying Bert Yancey for third place.

4:18 P.M.

Bert Yancey looks over his curling downhill six-footer and decides that he must hit it firmly to keep the ball from breaking too sharply. His stroke is firm, but still the ball breaks too much, and Yancey fails, by inches, to get the birdie that would have created a three-way tie for first place.

4:19 P.M.

Gene Littler gingerly strokes in a two-footer for a par on fourteen. Bert Yancey also picks up his par.

4:21 P.M.

Even his aqua shirt and his gold sweater can't brighten Larry Hinson. He comes off the eighteenth green with a disastrous 79, the highest round of the day. After three straight rounds of par or better, after starting the day in tenth place, Hinson staggers in at 294, too high, he discovers, even to make the top twenty-four.

Bob Lunn, playing with Hinson, finishes at 72 and 287.

4:25 P.M.

Putting from just off the back of the fourteenth green, Gary Player leaves his approach putt some seven or eight feet away from the cup. He shakes his head unhappily.

4:26 P.M.

From fourteen feet away, Billy Casper putts to within a foot of the hole and taps in for his par.

4:27 P.M.

Gary Player three-putts for a bogey on fourteen and tumbles to eight-under, deadlocked for second place with Billy Casper and Bert Yancey. Now Gene Littler is all alone in first place at nine-under.

4:28 P.M.

Both Gene Littler and Bert Yancey, untroubled by the new mounds, go for the fifteenth green with their second shots. Littler feels the proper shot for him is a two-iron, but he wants loft to try to hold the green. He takes his four-wood. Both men clear the water, but Yancey catches a bunker, and Littler's high shot still rolls off the back edge of the green.

4:31 P.M.

With a birdie on seventeen and a par on eighteen, Frank Beard comes in at 70 for 285, three-under. Among the players who have finished, he is second to Nicklaus. With only eight

April 12, 1970

players still on the course, Beard has wrapped up a spot in the top ten for the third time in six appearances at Augusta.

His playing partner, Takaaki Kono, comes in with a 74 and, for the second straight year, finishes at even-par 288. For Kono, it has been an off-day—not a single eagle.

4:32 P.M.

Troubled by a murderous lie under the lip of the bunker, Bert Yancey has no chance to blast out softly close to the pin on fifteen. He takes a full swing, and the ball sails nearly twenty feet beyond the hole.

4:33 P.M.

Gene Littler hits a magnificent chip shot from the back of the fifteenth green. The ball streaks straight for the hole, then stops, inches short of an eagle. Littler taps in for his birdie.

Suddenly, the traffic jam has eased. Gene Littler is the first player in the 1970 Masters to go ten under par. He is in front by two strokes.

4:34 P.M.

Bert Yancey two-putts for his tenth straight par and remains two strokes behind.

4:35 P.M.

None of the leaders is playing safe now, not with time running out. Back on the fifteenth fairway, Gary Player and Billy Casper both see Gene Littler score his birdie, both know that they must go for the green.

The two golfers both clear the water—the fears early in the week that the new mounds would make it almost impossible to reach fifteen in two have vanished in a trailing breeze—but both miss the slick green, and end up in sand.

4:37 P.M.

As Gene Littler steps to the par-three sixteenth, he figures that if he can par the last three holes, barring a Palmer-like charge by one of his rivals, he will be the Masters champion. He decides to play it safe, not to go for the pin, simply to cozy a shot onto the green. He is too gentle. He misses the green and lands in a bunker.

4:38 P.M.

This is Bert Yancey's hole, the sixteenth, and he realizes that if he can produce a birdie, and if Gene Littler bogeys, he will be tied for the lead. If Billy Casper and Gary Player both birdie the fifteenth, there will be a four-way tie for the lead.

Yancey fires at the pin, but his tee shot slides off the edge of the green, some thirty-five feet from the cup.

4:39 P.M.

Gary Player, whose performance out of bunkers all week has not been up to his usual brilliance, blasts out far short of the hole.

Then Billy Casper, who is considered more skilled at putting and chipping than sand play, blasts to within four feet of the pin.

4:41 P.M.

Dave Hill and Dave Stockton both come in at 70 and 283, five-under. "I'm finally over my fear of this course," says Stockton. "I know now that someday I can win here."

4:42 P.M.

Gene Litttler, one of the better sand players, comes out of the bunker on sixteen, and his ball stops fifteen feet from the hole.

4:43 P.M.

On the fifteenth, Gary Player two-putts for a par, and Billy Casper guides in his four-footer for a birdie and takes over second place, all alone at nine-under.

April 12, 1970

4:44 P.M.

Bert Yancey's bid for a birdie on sixteen rolls fully four feet past the cup, placing his par in jeopardy. "I thought it was going in," says Yancey.

4:45 P.M.

Gene Littler's bid for a par misses by inches. He taps in for a bogey, and in the space of two minutes, his two-stroke lead has evaporated. He is tied for the lead, with Billy Casper, at nine-under.

4:46 P.M.

The lower locker room is crowded with players and reporters watching the finishing holes on CBS. As Bert Yancey lines up his four-footer on sixteen, Tony Jacklin, his friend, says anxiously, "That's a crucial putt for him."

Then Yancey strokes the ball into the hole, and Jacklin lets out a cheer.

4:47 P.M.

Billy Casper and Gary Player step up to the sixteenth tee. Casper hits first, and his tee shot carries to the back fringe of the green. Player promptly strokes his shot to within eight feet of the cup.

4:48 P.M.

On the seventeenth hole, Gene Littler and Bert Yancey both hit perfect drives down the heart of the fairway.

4:49 P.M.

One of the CBS announcers, trying to explain how a four-way playoff is possible, gets twisted in his own words and stumbles over a few strokes. "Even the announcers are choking," says Tony Jacklin.

4:51 P.M.

Like Bert Yancey a few minutes ago, Billy Casper cannot hold his downhill putt on sixteen. He rolls four feet past the cup and faces a critical putt coming back.

4:52 P.M.

Not one golfer has birdied sixteen yet today. As Gary Player studies his uphill eight-footer, a cash register at a nearby concession stand clangs twice. Player ignores the sound, strokes the ball and watches it dive into the cup. He breaks into a big smile, and now, after seventy of seventy-two holes, the 1970 Masters has a three-way tie for the lead—Player, Billy Casper and Gene Littler—with Bert Yancey only one stroke behind.

4:53 P.M.

With body English and a smooth stroke, Billy Casper sends home his four-footer to preserve his par and his share of first place.

4:54 P.M.

Gene Littler and Bert Yancey both put their second shots on the green on seventeen, Yancey about thirty feet from the hole, Littler about fifteen.

4:55 P.M.

Tommy Aaron finishes, with a 72, at 283, tying Dave Hill and Dave Stockton for fifth place. Aaron's playing partner, Charlie Coody, struggles in with a 77 and 288.

"That does it," says Tony Jacklin, as he learns of Coody's even-par finish. He walks outside to his wife and, with a big grin, says, "I'm joint twelfth," which is British for tied for twelfth.

Jacklin turns to a reporter and adds, "You may think I'm overly excited, but the Masters is probably even bigger outside your country than in it, and this finish means a great deal to me and to the British people."

Then Jacklin returns to the "telly."

4:56 P.M.

Billy Casper hits a good drive on seventeen, Gary Player a poor one that leaves him with a blind shot of more than 150 yards to the green.

4:57 P.M.

Bert Yancey's approach putt dies a couple of feet from the seventeenth hole, and Yancey then rams in his twelfth consecutive par.

4:58 P.M.

Putting cautiously, never giving himself a chance for a birdie, Gene Littler leaves his ball almost a foot short of the cup. He taps in for his par and heads toward the eighteenth tee, still nine-under.

4:59 P.M.

Billy Casper puts his second shot six feet from the cup on seventeen and marches up the fairway with the look of a man who is about to collect a birdie.

With a remarkable recovery, Gary Player fires his second shot to the center of the green, a long way from the cup.

5 P.M.

Gene Littler and Bert Yancey both hit the eighteenth fairway with their drives.

5:03 P.M.

Gary Player's long putt ends up four feet from the hole.

5:04 P.M.

Gene Littler strokes his second shot to the eighteenth green, some twenty feet from the cup.

5:05 P.M.

A little more than 150 yards from the eighteenth green, Bert Yancey debates his club selection. He knows that he must get close enough for a birdie if he wants to tie Gene Littler. "It's either a little six or a big seven," he tells himself. "I'm charged up. I'll hit a seven."

Yancey's choice is wrong. He hits the seven-iron, and it simply isn't enough club. His shot falls into a bunker in front of the green. His face falls, too. Now, if his Masters dream is to come true, Yancey must hole out from the sand to gain a tie.

5:06 P.M.

The locker-room crowd is tense, watching Billy Casper measuring his six-footer on seventeen. "Tough putt," Tony Jacklin says. "It's a tough putt."

Casper gets set over his ball, then stops and stares at the crowd. Apparently, he has heard some noise. "He lets things like that bother him," says George Archer, the defending champion, watching the television screen.

Once again, Casper moves over the ball, and now he strokes it and the ball rushes up to the hole and breaks away. Casper, trying to wish the ball into the hole, twists his body and bends his knees almost to the ground.

"Here's your headline for a picture of that," says Archer, with a grin. "CASPER TO KNEES; LORD SAYS NO."

Casper taps in for a par and retains his share of the lead.

5:07 P.M.

"C'mon, Yance," Tom Weiskopf yells at the television screen. But the words don't help. Bert Yancey's explosion shot, his last chance, scoots past the hole.

April 12, 1970

5:08 P.M.

Gary Player sinks his four-footer for a par on seventeen, clutches his stomach and looks gratefully toward the sky. He remains nine-under, even with Billy Casper and Gene Littler.

5:09 P.M.

Billy Casper and Gary Player both drive long down the eighteenth fairway.

5:10 P.M.

Bert Yancey's putt for a par, almost meaningless now, hits the cup and slides by, and he accepts his first bogey of the day. Yancey walks off the green with a round of 70 and a total of 281.

5:11 P.M.

Gene Littler studies his twenty-footer on eighteen, and in the lower locker room, George Archer cheers, "The green frog!" Archer explains that "the green frog" is a good-luck expression used, he says, among baseball players. There are no baseball players around to contradict him.

Littler strokes his putt, too weak again, a foot or so short of the hole. "Gene," Archer tells the television screen, "that's no time to lag." Then, looking away from the screen, Archer adds, with understanding, not sarcasm, "I guess Gene got a little tight. He saw that scoreboard."

The scoreboard shows Littler in at nine-under, 279, and Billy Casper and Gary Player, with one hole to go, also at nine-under.

5:13 P.M.

Billy Casper and Gary Player stand in the eighteenth fairway, examining their second shots. Each picks his club, and Casper, perhaps fifteen yards closer to the hole, turns to watch Player's bid.

Casper, with a six-iron in his hand, sees that Player is getting set to hit a six-iron, too. "He better hit it hard," Casper thinks, "or he's not going to get up."

But Player is also thinking. He knows that a five-iron is the safer club, but he isn't interested in safety, in reaching the wide-open back level of the green. He doesn't care about second place. The South African realizes that Casper has a shot at a birdie, and he intends to go for a birdie, too. His only chance is to aim for the front of the green.

He swings into his six-iron and sends the ball flying straight toward the flag. But the six-iron isn't enough club. The ball lands in the same bunker that caught Bert Yancey's shot, the same bunker Player himself found nine years ago, when he got up and down in two and beat Arnold Palmer out of a green jacket.

5:14 P.M.

Billy Casper strokes his six-iron toward the center of the green and comes to rest ten feet above the hole, well within birdie range.

5:15 P.M.

Not everyone in the locker room is totally absorbed in the drama of the finish. Orville Moody, the U.S. Open champion, stands up and walks to his locker. "Want to get going to the airport," he asks a friend, "before the traffic starts?"

5:16 P.M.

Gary Player heads into the bunker to prepare for his third shot. Only a week ago, he was telling reporters how, in 1969, he had been in bunkers ninety-two times and had gotten up and down in two strokes eighty-four times.

Now he blasts out, and his shot takes one bounce, just misses hitting the pin and rolls about six and a half feet beyond the hole.

April 12, 1970

5:17 P.M.

Behind the green, Gene Littler watches Billy Casper lining up his ten-foot downhill birdie attempt. "He'll make it," Littler tells himself, matter-of-factly.

In the lower locker room, George Archer again calls, "The green frog!" Archer, who is wearing his champion's jacket, smiles. "I just want a winner," he says, "somebody I can put the green jacket on. I've got an exhibition in Atlanta tomorrow, and I don't want to have to come back here for a playoff."

Off the veranda, behind the Augusta National clubhouse, tables, chairs and microphone are all set up. Everything is ready for the Masters presentation ceremony, everything except a champion.

5:18 P.M.

"It's fast," Billy Casper tells himself, "and it's gonna break right." He aims four inches to the left of the cup, brings his putter back, then forward, and gently strokes the ball.

"It's in," Casper thinks.

His caddy, Matthew Palmer, tenses himself for an explosive cheer.

The ball runs up to the cup, teasingly kisses the lip and trickles away. Casper, again almost to his knees, jerks his head upward in disappointment.

"Well, that makes me the world's only six-foot-six coat-hanger," says George Archer.

Casper taps in for his par and finishes, even with Gene Littler, at 279.

5:19 P.M.

Now it is Gary Player's turn under extreme pressure. He walks around the green, studying his putt from all angles, then positions himself over the ball. A couple of movie cameras in the photographers' stand near the green begin to whir. Player backs away and glares at the stand. The cameras continue to roll.

Player addresses his putt once more and taps the ball. It rolls downhill, breaks toward the cup and breaks too much. Player's face falls; the ball slides by the hole.

The South African takes a bogey and, with no pleasure, wraps up third place, his best finish at Augusta in eight years, since he and Dow Finsterwald lost a three-way playoff to Arnold Palmer.

The scene is set for the sixth playoff in Masters history: Billy Casper vs. Gene Littler tomorrow.

5:25 P.M.

Bert Yancey reaches into his locker, pulls out a white leather bag, throws a few golfballs inside and zips it up. "Wrong judgment on sixteen, seventeen, and eighteen," he says, half to himself, half to the newspapermen circling him. "I thought I was getting all psyched up to charge, and I was just going blank."

Yancey shakes his head. "I played good all day," he says. "I played the best two rounds of my life the last two days. I played the best golf of my life and finished fourth and did it under pressure."

Yancey pauses. "It takes a lot to win this tournament," he says. "Look at Littler and Casper, the frustrations they've had here."

He turns to leave the locker room. "More and more each year," Bert Yancey says, "I realize what it means to win here. More and more, I appreciate what it takes. It'll make it sweeter when I do win."

5:40 P.M.

In the interview room, Gary Player faces the press. "Don't put too much emphasis on the last hole," he suggests. "The camera did bother me, but I messed up a few other holes, you know. It wasn't just the eighteenth.

"I putted so badly. The way I was putting and not getting down from the fringes, I was lucky to be so close."

April 12, 1970

Player reviews his round, then quietly adds, "It's a game of disappointment, isn't that right? One of *them* tomorrow will be sad, you know."

He nods to the reporters and gets up to walk from press headquarters to the locker room. He covers the full distance, perhaps a couple of hundred feet, with his head down, a cluster of writers following him. "You really gave it a go," one writer says, sympathetically.

"It was the finest golf I've ever played to lose a tournament," concedes Player, differentiating between his "play" and his putting. "I'd rather have lost by five shots than the way I did."

He stops and looks at the reporters. "My dad told me," Player says, "when I went into golf there would be good days and bad days. He said I've got to smile when things are going bad, so—look at my teeth."

And Gary Player, unsmiling, bares his teeth.

6:05 P.M.

Two men who grew up at the same time in the San Diego area and have been golfing rivals for more than twenty years— Billy Casper and Gene Littler—sit together in front of a band of reporters.

A week ago, when they both finished far from the lead at Greensboro, nobody had any questions for them.

"Well, Gene," says Casper, cheerfully, "it took us seventy-two holes to get rid of the other fellows."

Littler, as talkative as ever, nods pleasantly.

"We live about two good brassie shots away from each other," Casper says.

"More than that," says Littler, as honest as ever.

Someone asks Casper what he was thinking about before he tried for the birdie on eighteen, and Casper, as proper as ever says, "I was thinking, 'You can achieve a goal you have wanted to accomplish.'"

Someone else asks Littler about his unadventurous putts on

seventeen and eighteen. "I was chokin' like a dog," Littler admits.

"I'm grateful to be in a playoff," Casper reveals.

"Strange turn of events, my being here," says Littler. "I played so awful lately and so lousy in practice here." He rubs his head. "I don't know where I'll stay tonight," he adds. "I'm kicked out of my rented house. The owners came back today."

Will each of the Californians outline his strategy for tomorrow?

"I'll tee it high, and let it fly," says Casper, with a grin.

Littler gives Casper a quick glance. "I'll tee it low and let it go."

Littler, by consensus, wins the interview from Casper.

6:25 P.M.

Outside press headquarters, Shirley Casper is explaining her feelings to a reporter. "The Masters has been so elusive for us," she says. "I'm almost afraid to hope. It's very important to Bill. First of all, from a management standpoint. Winning the Masters will give us an early start on business promotions. And then, well, *pride*."

Mrs. Casper smiles. "To win the *Masters*," she says. "How do you put a dollar sign on *that*?"

6:45 P.M.

Billy Casper stands by his locker, speaking of "honest accomplishments" and "goals achieved," the sort of phrases he favors. "The really true test of a champion," he says, "is to accept defeat graciously."

6:50 P.M.

As they wait for Billy Casper to emerge from the locker room, young Billy turns to his mother. "Will Mr. Littler stay with us if he can't find a place?" the boy asks.

"I'm sure he'll find a place," says Shirley Casper.

April 12, 1970

THE TOP TWENTY-FOUR

Gene Littler	69-70-70-70—279
Billy Casper	72-68-68-71—279
Gary Player	74-68-68-70—280
Bert Yancey	69-70-72-70—281
Tommy Aaron	68-74-69-72—283
Dave Hill	73-70-70-70—283
Dave Stockton	72-72-69-70—283
Jack Nicklaus	71-75-69-69—284
Frank Beard	71-76-68-70—285
Bob Lunn	70-70-75-72—287
Juan Rodriguez	70-76-73-68—287
Charles Coody	70-74-67-77—288
Takaaki Kono	75-68-71-74—288
Tony Jacklin	73-74-70-71—288
Don January	76-73-69-70—288
Bert Greene	75-71-70-72—288
Bob Charles	75-71-71-72—289
Howie Johnson	75-71-73-71—290
Dick Lotz	74-72-72-72—290
Orville Moody	73-72-71-74—290
Miller Barber	76-73-77-65—291
Terry Wilcox	79-70-70-72—291
Deane Beman	74-72-72-74—292
Charles R. Coe	74-71-72-75—292
Julius Boros	75-71-74-72—292
Bob Murphy	78-70-73-71—292
Sam Snead	76-73-71-72—292
Tom Weiskopf	73-73-72-74—292

MONDAY

April 13, 1970

Out of the Woods

If the playoff between Billy Casper and Gene Littler could be pushed back in time some twenty years, to the days when they were both teenagers growing up in San Diego, there would be little suspense. Gene Littler would be an overwhelming favorite.

In those days, Littler was, by a sizable margin, the superior golfer of the two. He was, in fact, quite possibly the finest teenaged golfer in the world. "As good as he is right now," says Casper, "I believe Gene was a better player then. He was more consistent. If you think he hits the ball solidly now, you should have seen him then."

Littler and Casper faced each other a few times in high-school and junior-golf matches, and always, Littler, who was eleven months older, won. They never played for money, for a simple reason. "We didn't have any," explains Littler. For a while, they were teammates on the San Diego Naval Training Station golf team, and everyone who saw both of them play predicted a brighter career for Littler.

"Billy was always a great chipper and putter," says Littler, "but he wasn't a fine shotmaker then."

In 1953, when he was twenty-three years old, Gene Littler

won the U.S. Amateur championship. The following January, still an amateur, he won the San Diego Open, one of the few times an amateur has captured a tournament on the PGA tour. Littler promptly turned pro; the same year, Casper and, incidentally, Arnold Palmer followed him into the professional ranks, making it, in retrospect, a vintage year for golf. No one outside Southern California heard a word about Casper in 1954, but that June, when he was still only twenty-three, a rookie on the golf tour, Littler finished second, by a single stroke, in the U.S. Open.

He was accepted as the coming superstar of the sport, and in 1955, his first full year on tour, he fulfilled his promise. He won four tournaments and was the fifth-leading money-winner in the country. The same year, Casper didn't win a tournament and didn't even place among the top fifty money-winners.

In 1956, Littler's wide edge over Casper began to vanish. "Billy improved tremendously playing the tour," Littler recalls. "He learned to hit all his shots."

Through 1963, the end of their first decade as professionals, the two Southern Californians were just about equally successful. During that stretch, Casper won twenty-one tournaments and Littler nineteen, each earned close to $300,000 in prize money and each won the U.S. Open, Casper in 1959 and Littler in 1961. Each established his own image. Littler, quiet and calm, was known as a perfectionist, a man who sought to execute every shot precisely right. Casper, roly-poly, beset by frequent illnesses and occasional temper fits, was known, beyond all else, as an incredibly gifted putter, a designation that irritated him, because he felt that the rest of his game was being slighted.

After 1963, Casper pulled away from Littler, at least partly because Littler chose to spend less time on the tour. In 1966, not long after he found a diet that chased away his allergies and his excess weight, and only a few months after he joined the Mor-

April 13, 1970

mon Church, Casper won his second U.S. Open. In 1968, he became the first golfer in history to earn more than $200,000 in prize money in a single year. From 1964 through 1969, Casper won twenty-three tournaments and $700,000, and became the third-leading money-winner of all time. During the same period, Littler won three tournaments and $350,000, and became the fifth-leading money-winner of all time.

Casper was one of the superstars of golf, on a level with Arnold Palmer, Jack Nicklaus and Gary Player in skill, if not in gate appeal. Littler's stature was greater among his fellow players than among golf's fans; his smooth swing was an object of awe and envy.

Not since Ben Hogan and Byron Nelson came out of Fort Worth had one city produced two such brilliant golfers as Casper and Littler. Yet, at the start of April, 1970, they had, between them, participated in twenty-nine Masters tournaments and did not have a single victory to show.

That oversight, obviously, would be corrected by the end of today.

7:30 A.M.

Nine hours after he phoned his wife to tell her, as she already suspected, that he'd be a day late getting home to La Jolla, Gene Littler wakes up. The playoff is scheduled to begin in six and a half hours, at two o'clock, and he should have no difficulty getting to the first tee on time. He has to travel only a hundred yards. Littler has spent the night in a member's cottage—a twelve-room cottage—on the Augusta National grounds.

9:10 A.M.

Billy Casper lies in bed in his rented home in North Augusta, reading the sports pages of the Augusta morning paper. His wife is already busy in the kitchen, preparing breakfast for

Billy and his son and a few friends. Casper's breakfast, on play-off morning, is shrimp and avocados.

11:40 A.M.

Gene Littler, brown-haired and blue-eyed, walks into the Augusta National clubhouse. He is wearing a light-green short-sleeved shirt, bright-green slacks, green socks and black alligator loafers. "That outfit would sure go well with a green jacket," a newspaperman greets him.

Littler smiles. "Gonna be sticky today," he says.

He yawns. "Slept pretty good. Guess I wore myself out yesterday."

Singly, and in small groups, reporters drift into the clubhouse and are startled to find one of the contestants on hand so early. With nothing better to do, they pepper Littler with questions. "Haven't brought my family here," he says, "since we all traveled the road together. Over ten years ago. Probably 1958." He has two children, a sixteen-year-old boy named Curt and a twelve-year-old girl named Suzanne, and his wife, like Casper's, is named Shirley. "I call home every other night when I'm away," Littler says.

He answers the familiar questions simply and concisely, without enthusiasm or annoyance. "Billy and I weren't exactly neighbors," he says. "He grew up about fifteen miles south of San Diego, and I was about fifteen miles north."

Someone asks about his antique cars, and, briefly, Littler brightens. "I've got a 1914 Model T," he says, "and a 1924 Rolls Royce, a 1929 Rolls Royce and a 1939 Rolls Royce. Just one of them's in show condition. I fool around with them, and I drive one every day. I've got a Jaguar XKE the family uses."

The subject shifts to Littler's fourth round. "What happened on sixteen?" a reporter asks.

"I choked," Littler says. "Took a gutless swing. Just didn't go through and hit it. It was a shot I wouldn't have hit if I'd been a stroke behind."

"Were you nervous?"

April 13, 1970

Littler looks surprised. "Anybody who says he's not nervous coming down to the last three holes," he says, "is kidding himself or kidding the public."

The questions continue, and Littler fields them all. "You enjoy these interviews?" someone asks.

"Not especially," says Honest Gene.

12:25 P.M.

Curt Bushman, representing Uni-Managers Incorporated, which represents Billy Casper, stands outside the clubhouse with Casper's son. "What's the Masters worth to Casper if he wins it?" someone asks.

"A good million in endorsements," says Bushman.

"Is Casper aware of that?"

"You bet he is," says Bushman.

12:45 P.M.

Wearing a blue turtleneck shirt, a red sweater and black-and-white checkered slacks, Billy Casper enters the clubhouse and nods hello to Gene Littler. "Think we can get penalized for slow play today, Gene?" says Casper, pleasantly.

As Casper moves to his locker, the reporters turn to follow him, and Littler, grateful for the opportunity to escape, heads out toward the practice tee.

"When Gene was a teenager," Casper says, "he could shoot a 64 any time he walked on a course. These days, he doesn't seem to hit so many crisp and solid shots. It looks like he's always trying something, always experimenting." Casper shakes his head, as if he is already feeling sorry for his opponent.

1:15 P.M.

On the practice tee, Billy Casper is swinging easily, casually, hitting half a dozen balls with each club in his bag, paying little attention to where each shot goes. Only a few drastic hooks seem to concern him at all.

"I'll bet you're out of that sweater by the second hole," a friend calls.

"No sir," says Casper. "I'll have it on all the way. I like to get a good sweat going and then keep it going. A lot of people make a mistake this way. You sweat a little and take off the sweater, then you stand in the shade for a few minutes and you cool down too fast. You can lose your momentum that way. Unless it's terribly hot, I always wear a sweater."

1:45 P.M.

As Gene Littler comes off the practice tee, a reporter, desperately searching for an angle, asks, "Gene, do you have any religious affiliation?"

Littler pauses, perhaps wondering if the question is serious. "Well," he says, finally, "I'm a Lutheran."

"I'll try to make something out of that," the reporter says.

"Be my guest," says Littler.

Another reporter, overhearing the dialogue, chimes in, "Say, what's the record for Masters playoffs between Lutherans and Mormons?"

1:55 P.M.

A few hundred people are clustered around the practice green, watching Billy Casper and Gene Littler putt. The crowd applauds every putt that drops in. The first fairway is already lined with spectators, and the first green encircled.

More than 10,000 fans are on hand to watch the playoff for the San Diego city championship.

2:10 P.M.

Ten minutes behind schedule, Gene Littler steps to the first tee, takes two practice swings and powers his drive more than 275 yards down the fairway.

Billy Casper moves up and, using the new clubs he loves, lashes his drive fifteen or twenty yards beyond Littler's.

Shirley Casper, wearing a pink A-line dress and a pink

April 13, 1970

Pucci scarf, her right hand clenched in a fist, half-walks, half-trots to get into position to watch her husband's second shot. Her son and Curt Bushman follow her.

2:14 P.M.
After Gene Littler puts his second shot within sixteen feet of the hole, Billy Casper takes a wedge and lofts his ball straight toward the flag. "Bite, bite, bite," his son shouts.
The ball bites, and dies six feet from the cup.

2:21 P.M.
Gene Littler two-putts for his par, and as Billy Casper lines up his birdie attempt, a baby begins to cry near the green. Shirley Casper, standing not far from the baby, tenses. Then the baby is carried away, and Shirley Casper relaxes, and her husband, using a mallet-head putter, rolls in his birdie-three.
Casper goes one-up.

2:23 P.M.
Now Billy Casper has the honors, and he steps up to the second tee and hooks his drive, drastically, just as he had hooked some shots on the practice tee, and the ball flies into the tall pine trees lining the fairway.
Gene Littler drives safely down the middle.

2:26 P.M.
Billy Casper is in trouble. His ball is deep in the woods. He has a fairly good lie, but his path toward the green is blocked by a row of towering pines. Most of the dozens of spectators surrounding him in the woods assume that Casper will simply chip out into the fairway and surrender any chance to reach the green with his third shot.
But Casper keeps studying the straight line to the green, the dangerous route over the pines. "Are you going to try to go over the trees?" a Masters official asks.
"Yes," says Casper.
"Let's get those people out of there," the official yells

toward the pines. "We don't want anyone down there getting hit with a ball if it hits the trees."

Casper ignores the pessimism. He reaches into his red-and-white golf bag and pulls out a nine-iron. "Ain't no way he's gonna get the ball up over those trees," a spectator whispers.

Casper addresses his ball, testing his footing. "All right, Bill?" the Masters official asks.

Casper takes a practice swing. "Yes," he says. "Everything's OK."

Then, without any hesitation, Casper swings into the shot, lifts the ball perfectly, carries the pines comfortably and comes to rest in the fairway. He is still 175 yards from the second green, but he has pulled off an incredible pressure shot.

Gene Littler fires his second shot into ideal position, only thirty yards short of the green.

2:30 P.M.

Billy Casper's third shot flies off the back of the green, dimming his chances for a par. If Gene Littler can place his simple third shot close to the hole, he ought to pick up at least one stroke, possibly two.

Littler studies his little chip, steps up to the ball, swings and, inexplicably, like any Sunday duffer, shanks his shot into a bunker.

"He tried to cozy it up," says Shirley Casper.

Littler blasts out and leaves himself twenty feet from the cup, Casper chips within two feet, Littler two-putts for a bogey and Casper strokes in his par. Suddenly, just a few minutes after he was hidden in the woods and seemed certain to lose his lead, Casper is out of the woods and two strokes in front.

2:45 P.M.

With Clifford Roberts, the tournament chairman, standing on a golf cart to watch the action, Gene Littler knocks his second shot over the third green and Billy Casper puts his thirty-five feet from the hole.

April 13, 1970

After Littler neatly chips back to within four feet, Casper consults with his caddy, Matthew Palmer, then sends his long putt straight into the cup for a birdie-three. Littler saves his par, but now, after three holes, he is three strokes behind.

2:55 P.M.

Neither man hits the fourth green with his tee shot, but Billy Casper—for the fourth straight hole—takes only one putt, and Gene Littler needs two. Casper's par widens his lead to four strokes.

"If this keeps up for ten holes," Casper's son says, happily, "we can shake hands and go home."

"Don't you say that," snaps Shirley Casper. "Don't you *think* it."

3:08 P.M.

Both men par the fifth hole.

In 1942, the last time two men from the same town met in a playoff for the Masters championship, Ben Hogan led Byron Nelson by three strokes after five holes. Hogan then played the next eleven holes in one under par—and lost five strokes to Nelson.

Nelson won the playoff, 69 to 70.

3:12 P.M.

Billy Casper's tee shot is short of the sixth green, and as he prepares to chip up, a spectator clicks a camera. Casper turns and glares.

"Isn't that something?" says Shirley Casper. "That's awful."

After her husband chips to within three feet and, of course, one-putts to match Gene Littler's par, Shirley Casper walks over to a Pinkerton and points out the spectator with the camera.

The Pinkerton confiscates the camera. He tells the spectator that the camera can be picked up after the playoff.

3:25 P.M.

"Get in the hole, get in the hole," thirteen-year-old Billy Casper screams, and his father's eight-foot birdie putt obediently dives into the cup. Gene Littler two-putts from the same distance on the seventh green and falls five full strokes off Casper's pace. The 1970 Masters championship, with eleven holes to play, seems settled.

3:38 P.M.

On the eighth hole, Billy Casper and Gene Littler both two-putt for pars.

3:48 P.M.

On the ninth hole, Billy Casper and Gene Littler both take pars. Halfway through the playoff, Casper is at 33, three under par, and Littler is at 38, two-over.

In the 1962 playoff for the Masters championship, Arnold Palmer gained six strokes on the back nine to overtake Gary Player and earn the third of his four Masters titles.

3:50 P.M.

Between nines, Curt Bushman and young Billy Casper run into the clubhouse for Cokes. "All over?" a reporter says to Bushman.

"You're not going to get me to say that," says Bushman, warily.

3:52 P.M.

Now, after his drive on the tenth hole, Gene Littler is in the woods, but, unlike Billy Casper on the second hole, Littler does not escape easily. After his second shot, he is still in the woods. His club caught a branch on his back swing.

3:59 P.M.

Billy Casper bogeys the tenth hole—and still gains a stroke on Gene Littler, who double-bogeys to soar four over par. "I

April 13, 1970

think," a Masters official says to Shirley Casper, "that Gene wishes he were on the beach at La Jolla."

"We'll see," says Mrs. Casper.

4:11 P.M.

With a fourteen-foot birdie putt on the eleventh hole, Billy Casper moves back to three-under—and seven strokes in front of Gene Littler. Never in Masters history has there been such a one-sided playoff.

Hundreds of spectators drift away from the play. The drama is gone.

4:13 P.M.

A private drama is going on inside the CBS truck, the control center for the television production. The playoff is going on the air in seventeen minutes, which seems about two hours too late to capture any suspense.

Bill MacPhail, the head of CBS sports, listens to the intercom conversations among his people.

"This is going to be a real test, Frank," someone says to Frank Chirkinian, the director, "to make this sound like the Masters."

"Well," asks another announcer, "is it safe to say Gene Littler is a shoo-in for second?"

"He may finish third," someone answers.

"How much time till I'm on?" asks Ray Scott, positioned at the tower near the eighteenth green. "If I'm going to come on breathless, I'm going to have to run up and down the stairs a few times."

4:21 P.M.

After an errant tee shot, Billy Casper bogeys the twelfth hole. Gene Littler picks up his par and trails by six strokes.

4:24 P.M.

"Six minutes to annihilation," says a CBS announcer.

4:36 P.M.

Forced to gamble, Gene Littler reaches the thirteenth green in two and two-putts for a birdie. Billy Casper, the conservative now, hits his third shot onto the green and two-putts for a par. Littler is now one stroke ahead on television—and five strokes behind in the match.

4:49 P.M.

Gene Littler's birdie putt on fourteen barely misses, but for the third straight hole, he gains a stroke on Billy Casper. A bogey drops Casper to one-under for the day, still four shots in front of Littler.

"Don't worry," a friend says to Shirley Casper. "He's got a nice lead. He isn't going to lose it."

"I've seen it happen before," says Mrs. Casper.

5:03 P.M.

Pumped up, and charging, Gene Littler rifles a two-iron to the fifteenth green, and Billy Casper, unwilling to concede a stroke, goes for the green, too, and misses. He lands in a bunker next to the putting surface. Casper blasts out, leaving himself some twenty feet beyond the pin.

Littler lines up a forty-footer, shooting for an eagle. He aims and fires—and, by inches, misses. Shirley Casper bows her head and clenches both fists.

Casper two-putts for a par, Littler taps in for a birdie and, with three holes to play, the margin is now three strokes.

CBS, running in luck, has found itself a drama.

5:05 P.M.

Gene Littler, up first, hits his tee shot on sixteen to the left fringe of the green, perhaps thirty feet from the cup.

For the first time since the second hole, Billy Casper feels he is under pressure. He knows that Littler is in position for a par, and he knows, too, that if he should falter—if he should

April 13, 1970

hit his tee shot into the water protecting the green—he could lose two strokes of his three-stroke advantage.

He takes his five-iron and strokes it smoothly and comes up eight feet from the hole.

"Oh, beauty, beauty, beauty," says Shirley Casper.

5:09 P.M.

Boldly, Gene Littler goes for the cup. His thirty-foot putt runs up, hits the edge of the hole and slides four feet past.

Henry Longhurst, the British expert, is reporting on the sixteenth hole for CBS. "We wait," says Longhurst, in reverential tones, "for what could be the killer by Casper."

5:10 P.M.

Billy Casper looks over his eight-footer, examining the terrain from every angle. He turns to his caddy. "What do you think?" Casper asks.

"Straight in," says Matthew Palmer.

"Are you sure?" Casper asks. There aren't many straight-in putts at Augusta National.

Matthew Palmer nods.

Casper sets himself over the ball, steadies himself and putts. The ball heads straight toward the hole.

"It's going in the hole," young Billy Casper shouts. "It's going in the hole. It's going in the hole!"

The ball goes in the hole.

Young Billy kisses his mother, and Curt Bushman, the agent, raises his fist over his head like a winning fighter.

The Masters playoff, for all practical purposes, is over. Even though Gene Littler salvages his par, Casper is four strokes ahead with only two holes to play.

5:11 P.M.

Just as Billy Casper's putt disappears into the cup, George Archer, the outgoing Masters champion, walks into the Augusta National clubhouse, freshly returned from his exhibition in Atlanta.

"I think he wants to win," says Archer, studying Casper's happy reaction to the birdie.

Archer turns away from the television screen and walks to the coat rack to get the new green jacket he will present to the 1970 Masters champion.

5:16 P.M.

Walking along the seventeenth fairway, Mannie Neikrie, a friend of the Casper family, shakes his head. "Shirley almost had a nervous breakdown on fifteen," he says.

"I know," says Curt Bushman. "It's more Nicklaus and Palmer she's playing than Littler. They have this title, and she doesn't."

Casper birdies the seventeenth, Littler bogeys and they move to the final tee six strokes apart.

5:29 P.M.

After seventeen frustrating holes, Gene Littler finally sinks a decent birdie putt—a twelve-footer—his thirty-sixth putt of the day and his 166th of the 1970 Masters tournament.

Billy Casper's two putts—for a par—give him twenty-seven putts for the round and 145 for the tournament, an average of only 1.6 putts per twisting, treacherous green. Not once in the entire ninety holes of competition did Casper three-putt.

He comes in with a 69 and a five-stroke margin of victory.

5:31 P.M.

"I feel very grateful to Gene for getting off to a bad start," says Billy Casper. "That made it a lot easier."

5:33 P.M.

"I was beaten," says Gene Littler. "I have no excuses."

5:36 P.M.

"If it weren't for my caddy," Billy Casper tells the press, "I wouldn't be here. He helped me read every green, one, two,

April 13, 1970

three, right on through eighteen. Now he tells me he's thinking of changing his name to Matthew Casper."

5:40 P.M.

Matthew Palmer, who has caddied for Billy Casper in the last six Masters, is entertaining the press.

"Billy says you helped him a lot," someone says.

"We got help from up above," Palmer replies. "I've got to give him the credit. I can't hit the ball for him. If I did, we'd have about a million shots."

"How does it feel to caddy for the Masters champion?"

"It feels wonderful," Palmer says, "but, remember, I didn't hit any shots."

"How do you read the greens?"

"How do you do your job?" says Matthew Palmer. "Reading greens is my job. I'm interested. Sure, I play golf, but my handicap's about twenty. Golf's not my game. Knowing about golf is my game."

Palmer is so modest he may be drummed out of the caddy corps.

Neither Casper nor Palmer reveals exactly how much the caddy will receive, but sometimes, when he wins a tournament, Casper gives ten per cent of his prize money to his caddy. That means, this week, perhaps $2,500 for Matthew Palmer—and a $2,500 tithe for the Mormon Church.

5:58 P.M.

George Archer, the first Californian to win the Masters, drapes the green jacket on the second, Billy Casper. Naturally, the jacket doesn't fit. It is practically Melnyk-size, far too large for Casper. "I think," he says, "they must have measured me the first time I played here—fourteen years ago."

But, too large or not, Billy Casper quickly wraps himself inside the green symbol of the 1970 Masters championship.

Appendix

THE 1970 MASTERS

PLAYER	FINISH	SCORE	PRIZE MONEY
Billy Casper, Jr. LOW PROFESSIONAL: *Sterling replica of Masters trophy* *Gold medal* *Silver cigarette box engraved with the names of all the 1970 entrants* *Crystal vase for low score, April 10 (68-tie)*	1	72 68 68 71 279*	$25,000
Gene Littler RUNNER-UP: *Silver medal*	2	69 70 70 70 279	$17,500
Gary Player *Crystal vase for low score, April 10 (68-tie)*	3	74 68 68 70 280	$14,000
Bert Yancey	4	69 70 72 70 281	$10,000
Tommy Aaron *Crystal vase for low score, April 9 (68)*	T-5	68 74 69 72 283	$ 6,667
Dave Hill	T-5	73 70 70 70 283	$ 6,667
Dave Stockton	T-5	72 72 69 70 283	$ 6,667
Jack Nicklaus *Pair of crystal goblets, eagle, No. 15, April 11* *Pair of crystal goblets, eagle, No. 2, April 12*	8	71 75 69 69 284	$ 4,500
Frank Beard *Pair of crystal goblets, eagle, No. 2, April 11*	9	71 76 68 70 285	$ 4,000
Bob Lunn	T-10	70 70 75 72 287	$ 3,500
Juan Rodriguez	T-10	70 76 73 68 287	$ 3,500

*Won playoff, 69-74.

Appendix

PLAYER	FINISH	SCORE	PRIZE MONEY
Charles Coody *Crystal vase for low score,* April 11 (67)	T-12	70 74 67 77 288	$ 3,000
Bert Greene	T-12	75 71 70 72 288	$ 3,000
Tony Jacklin (*England*)	T-12	75 71 70 72 288	$ 3,000
Don January *Pair of crystal goblets,* *eagle,* No. 15, April 12	T-12	76 73 69 70 288	$ 3,000
Takaaki Kono (*Japan*) *Crystal vase for low score,* April 10 (68-tie) *Pair of crystal goblets,* *eagle,* No. 1, April 11	T-12	75 68 71 74 288	$ 3,000
Bob Charles (*New Zealand*)	17	75 71 71 72 289	$ 2,700
Howie Johnson	T-18	75 71 73 71 290	$ 2,500
Dick Lotz	T-18	74 72 72 72 290	$ 2,500
Orville Moody	T-18	73 72 71 74 290	$ 2,500
Miller Barber *Crystal vase for low score,* April 12 (65)	T-21	76 73 77 65 291	$ 2,250
Terry Wilcox	T-21	79 70 70 72 291	$ 2,250
Deane Beman	T-23	74 72 72 74 292	$ 2,020
Charles Coe LOW AMATEUR: *Gold-silver cup* *Gold medal* *Silver cigarette box engraved* *with the names of all* *amateur entrants*	T-23	74 71 72 75 292	Amateur
Julius Boros *Pair of crystal goblets,* *eagle,* No. 13, April 12	T-23	75 71 74 72 292	$ 2,020
Bob Murphy	T-23	78 70 73 71 292	$ 2,020
Sam Snead	T-23	76 73 71 72 292	$ 2,020
Tom Weiskopf	T-23	73 73 72 74 292	$ 2,020

Appendix

PLAYER	FINISH	SCORE	PRIZE MONEY
Jimmy Wright	T-29	75 72 71 75 293	$ 1,650
Hsieh Yung-Ho (*Nationalist China*)	T-29	75 75 69 74 293	$ 1,650
George Archer	T-31	73 72 74 75 294	$ 1,650
Gay Brewer, Jr. *Pair of crystal goblets, eagle, No. 2, April 9 Pair of crystal goblets, eagle, No. 2, April 11 Pair of crystal goblets, eagle, No. 13, April 12*	T-31	78 70 72 74 294	$ 1,650
Bruce Devlin (*Australia*)	T-31	72 74 78 70 294	$ 1,650
Larry Hinson	T-31	72 72 71 79 294	$ 1,650
Ken Still	T-31	74 73 73 74 294	$ 1,650
Arnold Palmer	T-36	75 73 74 73 295	$ 1,575
Dan Sikes	T-36	70 77 71 77 295	$ 1,575
Maurice Bembridge (*England*)	T-38	77 72 70 77 296	$ 1,575
Bruce Crampton (*Australia*)	T-38	75 71 75 75 296	$ 1,575
Dale Douglass	T-38	76 74 72 74 296	$ 1,575
Marvin Giles, III AMATEUR RUNNER-UP: *Silver medal for amateur runner-up*	T-38	78 72 72 74 296	Amateur
Grier Jones	T-38	73 75 73 75 296	$ 1,575
Steven Melnyk	43	73 76 71 77 297	Amateur
Bob Rosburg	44	77 73 75 73 298	$ 1,500
Al Geiberger	T-45	73 77 74 75 299	$ 1,500
George Knudson (*Canada*) *Pair of crystal goblets, eagle, No. 15, April 12*	T-45	73 72 78 76 299	$ 1,500
R. H. Sikes	47	70 75 77 78 300	$ 1,500
Dean Refram	48	76 74 78 75 303	$ 1,500

Appendix

PLAYER	FINISH	SCORE	PRIZE MONEY
PLAYERS WHO DID NOT MAKE THE CUT-OFF (150)			
Bernard Gallacher (*Scotland*)		77 74 151	$ 1,000
Harold Henning (*South Africa*)		74 77 151	$ 1,000
Bunky Henry		77 74 151	$ 1,000
Dave Marr		75 76 151	$ 1,000
Roberto de Vicenzo (*Argentina*)		78 73 151	$ 1,000
Jerry Wadkins		79 72 151	Amateur
Ray Floyd		76 76 152	$ 1,000
William Hyndman, III		76 76 152	$ 1,000
Mason Rudolph		76 76 152	$ 1,000
Edgar Updegraff		78 74 152	Amateur
Art Wall, Jr.		76 76 152	$ 1,000
Kermit Zarley		74 78 152	$ 1,000
Lionel Hebert		75 78 153	$ 1,000
Cary Middlecoff		78 75 153	$ 1,000
Thomas Watson		77 76 153	$ 1,000
Peter Butler (*England*)		82 72 154	$ 1,000
John Farquhar		74 80 154	$ 1,000
Larry Ziegler		76 78 154	$ 1,000
Homero Blancas		81 74 155	$ 1,000
Doug Ford		76 79 155	$ 1,000
Bob Goalby		77 78 155	$ 1,000
Gene Sarazen		81 74 155	$ 1,000
Robert Zender		77 78 155	Amateur
Joseph Inman, Jr.		77 79 156	Amateur
Richard Siderowf		80 76 157	Amateur
Allen Miller, III		81 76 157	Amateur
Phil Rodgers		78 79 157	$ 1,000
Herman Keiser		79 79 158	$ 1,000
Jackie Burke, Jr.		78 80 158	$ 1,000
John Bohmann		81 78 159	Amateur
Roberto Bernardini (*Italy*)		80 80 160	$ 1,000
Michael Bonallack (*England*)		75 86 161	Amateur

Appendix

PLAYER	FINISH	SCORE	PRIZE MONEY
Sukree Onsham (*Thailand*)		78 84 162	$ 1,000
Ralph Guldahl		84 83 167	$ 1,000
Henry Picard		No Card	$ 1,000

PRESENT—DID NOT PARTICIPATE

Ben Hogan			$ 1,000
Byron Nelson			$ 1,000

HONORARY INVITEES

Jerry Barber			$ 500
Jim Ferrier			$ 500
Dow Finsterwald			$ 500
John W. Fischer, Jr.			Amateur
Jack Fleck			$ 500
Ed Furgol			$ 500
Vic Ghezzi			$ 500
Robert Hamilton			$ 500
M. R. (Chick) Harbert			$ 500
Jock Hutchison			$ 500
Fred McLeod			$ 500
Tony Manero			$ 500
Sam Parks, Jr.			$ 500
Denny Shute			$ 500
Jess W. Sweetser			Amateur
Jim Turnesa			$ 500
Lew Worsham, Jr.			$ 500
Charles R. Yates			Amateur

About the Author

DICK SCHAAP, former city editor and syndicated columnist for the New York *Herald Tribune*, has authored and edited more than a dozen books, including *Turned On, RFK, Instant Replay* (with Jerry Kramer), *I Can't Wait Until Tomorrow... 'Cause I Get Better-Looking Every Day* (with Joe Namath) and *PRO* (with Frank Beard).